AGILE PRODUCT OWNERSHIP

A Guide to Leading Agile Teams and Creating Great Products

BART GERARDI

Agile Product Ownership

A Guide to Leading Agile Teams and Creating Great Products

Bart Gerardi

Agile Product Ownership: A Guide to Leading Agile Teams and Creating Great Products

Second Edition, June 2014

To Judy,
for allowing me to continue to do this in the first place

Introduction

Thousands of books have been written about Agile software development and Agile project management. In nearly every one of these books, mention is made of the importance of the product owner, and how without this third piece to the puzzle the whole scheme falls apart. In fact, some of the literature will tell you that if you don't have a good product owner, you might as well abandon Agile as a concept; your results will be disappointing without one.

However, that's generally all the guidance that these books provide. Few of them discuss what a product owner is meant to do or how they are supposed to do it. It's as if the developers are unwilling to tell the business how to be good partners and hold up their end of the bargain. Perhaps the developers are fatigued from years of having the business tell them how to write software. This leaves our would-be product owners in a bad spot; they understand the role is important, but they don't understand the role itself.

This is a glaring weakness in the community at present. The need for quality product owners is vital to the success of the whole movement, yet the role is being overlooked. This book is a modest attempt to fill some of that void.

As someone who has been involved in Agile practices for a decade, the transition has been remarkable. When we first started out, the project manager or a senior engineer would play the role of product owner. They would talk with the business and try their best to understand the market, the needs and the goals of the project, and then they would play the role by proxy. At the time, this was actually helpful. The project manager usually had the business acumen to play the role, and they had the right mindset to do the work. Additionally, they were dedicated to the project anyway, so there weren't a lot of organizational issues to overcome. But while this was better than not having anyone in the role, it became apparent that it wasn't better than having the right person in the role.

Let's look at some key differences in product ownership in an Agile world.

Distributed vs. centralized ownership. In a non-Agile effort, the ownership of the product is generally distributed. Someone owns the product, while another person owns the marketing of it. Still a third may own the branding, while a fourth owns maintaining it. All told, there can be a dozen people who believe they own a piece of the product, from supply chain to delivery to service. With an Agile product, ownership of everything is centralized. The product owner owns the whole thing and they make all the decisions. This means that trade-offs that were almost impossible to evaluate in the past are now achievable. For instance, in the past, deciding to spend resources on improved packaging or on customer support was the kind of decision that would take dozens of people and hundreds of hours to adjudicate. In Agile, the product owner can make the decision however they want, and their decision is final.

Functional separation vs. cross-functional alignment. In the past, the business leadership of the product would be separate from the developers working on the product.

Communication would be done through documentation, would happen slowly, and be full of policies, politics, and misunderstandings. This would be exacerbated by the number of functions involved, generally at an exponential rate. If you had marketing, product, manufacturing and development involved in your product, then the communication could be 16 times more inefficient than it should be. In Agile, the team is the team – everyone is on the team, and communication is meant to be instantaneous, direct and open. Ideally, the whole team would be physically collocated, and a cross-functional discussion would merely require everyone standing up from their desk. But more importantly, the whole team is logically collocated; while they may be in different buildings, they are all on the same team. Experience has shown that makes all the difference.

Up-Front planning vs. constant planning. It's a canard to believe that Agile recommends performing no up-front planning, research and analysis. Where the two approaches differ is in the amount and the timing that these activities are executed. In a traditional methodology, years of effort and study would go into a product before it was ever even attempted to be built. The requirements and specifications would be decided and would be fixed before work began, and then the team would go off and build the product based on this years-old specification. Changes would be difficult or outright discouraged. In Agile, enough work is done before the team engages to know the direction and the general vision of what is to be built. This plan then is adjusted along the way, even right up to launch, and the team and process welcome and embrace these changes. This means that the people doing the analysis remain engaged through the development lifecycle, and it allows them to learn things along the way.

Big-Bang release vs. frequent releases and customer feedback. There have been several big-bang releases in the last few decades that have been very successful. At the same time there have been hundreds or thousands that have failed miserably. Agile makes it so that you don't need to be superlatively brilliant (or lucky) merely to succeed. By constantly releasing, the product owner is able to incorporate market and customer feedback in a rapid fashion. This allows the product to mature and better serve the needs of the customers without having to wait for another full product release cycle, perhaps missing the window on the market entirely.

Traditional methods teach the team to fear change; it will delay the product and will cause stress and possibly irreparable damage to the project. Agile teaches the team to embrace change, as it is the only possible path to success. The revision cycle for products is getting shorter and shorter. Waiting two years – or even six months – for a new version or update to your favorite product is no longer acceptable. Companies need to adapt to this new reality, and they need to choose a methodology that supports it. It is this reality that Agile was built for; if everyone was exactly right the first time, we would keep doing things the way we always have. Agile recognizes that this has never been the case, and provides for a way to navigate an ever changing environment.

Purpose of the Book

The purpose of this book is to better clarify the role of Agile Product Owner. This information is valuable to anyone who is interested in taking on the role of product owner, as well as anyone involved in an Agile project at all. We will also cover bits and pieces of Agile Project Management, and the Agile methodology in general. However, the focus will be on product ownership, and will cover topics such as:

- Product vision
- Creating and maintaining a product backlog
- Release planning and tracking
- Using meetings effectively
- Differences between traditional and Agile product ownership

This guide should allow for a framework to properly execute the role of product owner in many flavors of Agile, from Scrum to Kanban, XP to Lean. We will focus on software development projects, but the principles hold true for most products in just about every industry.

This book will certainly be valuable to those who find themselves managing Agile projects, but project management will not be the focus. It's also not intended to be an introduction to Agile; the book will assume that you are at least passingly familiar with most of the concepts and terminology. It's not intended to be a comprehensive treatise on product management; there are many aspects of good product management that won't be covered, such as how to do market research, how to do analysis, etc. This book is going to cover how a good product owner interacts with an Agile team to deliver a valuable product.

The aim of this book is to instruct product owners what it means to be a product owner in an Agile sense, and how to use the role to create and ship great products. In the end, that's what it's all about, right?

About the Author

Bart Gerardi is a program manager for an e-commerce company in the Ecommerce 50. He has been a consultant, manager, and leader for 18 years. Bart's love of bringing projects to market has spanned several companies, positions, and waves of Internet fads. Always on the lookout for new projects to run, he also manages the delivery of several teams bringing the next generation of e-commerce to the industry. Bart lives in the Seattle area.

Chapter 1

The Role of Product Owner

Let's start off with a story. In my first company, several years before the Agile Manifesto was written, I worked for a computer hardware company that was doing a major upgrade to its finance systems. The upgrade was meant to be purely technical and performance-improving in nature, as we were moving the systems off of legacy hardware and platforms, and onto shiny new ones. We were working off the most basic of all specifications: make it work exactly the way it currently works, only faster. We spent 18 months doing this, and by all accounts, we were successful. We ran both systems for over six months to ensure they were giving the same information, we did performance testing during the middle of the week and at a quarter close period, and we spot checked all reports to make sure everything was accurate. Every test past, every check succeeded.

But the project failed.

Two things had happened. Since the project was being run by engineering, there was very little outward communications. Eighteen months of development had gone by, and people's expectations kept climbing higher and higher, and no one was managing them. After all the wait, when the customers discovered that the system was really just a faster version of the exact same system, they were very disappointed. And second, this wasn't really a new product at all. There were no new features, no upgrades to existing features, and very few new elements, fixes or improvements. In fact, we made the decision to leave a few bugs in the system, because we wanted to match the old system as closely as possible. Worse than that, we painstakingly rebuilt, tested and deployed functionality that no one needed any longer, and no one would use. The product had no vision of its users, and never received any feedback along the way.

You can probably see where this is heading. A product without an owner is almost certainly doomed to disappoint in the marketplace. Without an owner, there is no vision, there is no mechanism for feedback and inspection, and there isn't anyone to properly prioritize functionality, or even to decide when to ship. As it was, our vision was to do nothing new, we never sought feedback, and we didn't ship till it was entirely complete. We failed.

Scrum, a flavor of Agile, says that the product owner is the one and only person responsible for deciding what to do next, and for ensuring a proper return on the work of the team. This person maintains the list of things to do (called a backlog) and is the only person who can decide when the product is ready either to release, or to be shown to customers to gain feedback. In some of the Agile literature, this definition is described in shorthand: the product owner is responsible for building the right product.

This means that the product owner leads the entire effort towards building a product that will be a success in the market. This includes crafting the vision for the product, finding the market, doing the analysis, planning the features, approving the releases, gaining feedback from users and customers, managing the budget, schedule and quality, and managing the launch or launches of the product itself. It also means full collaboration with the team, attending meetings, writing documents, and managing stakeholders. In other words, it's a big job, and the best practice is to have one and only one person doing it.

In many instances, not only is the product owner responsible for launching the product, but they are also given long-term responsibility for the full product lifecycle. This is meant to foster long-term planning, continuity in vision, and preventing loss of direction and momentum due to switching leaders mid-stream. The product owner is a part of the development team, as well as a part of the business team. It's a role that fully straddles both worlds, and as such, is a challenging role indeed.

I suspect right now, you are thinking that the product owner sounds a like product manager who also does some project management, or like a project manager who does some product management. While it is comfortable to think in these terms, it wouldn't be correct to do so. The product owner role is new role that is different than either of the two.

The product owner is responsible for the whole product, not just the development or the commercial success. This means that the product owner cannot abdicate decision making in functions where they feel they have no experience. If a product has hardware, software, manufacturing, distribution and a TV commercial, then the product owner owns all of it. This means that the amount of skill and the amount of accountability in the job is orders of magnitude more than any organization in the past.

No longer can the product owner act as adversary, and blame other functions for failures or under-performance. All credit for under or over-performance of the product goes to the product owner. This means that they need to be involved, they need to be highly skilled, and above all else, they need to care about every facet of the product.

The makings of a good Product Owner

It's fair to note that choosing a qualified product owner is critical to the success of any Agile project. The qualities that you want in a good product owner differ from what you might expect from a business owner, project sponsor, or project manager. Seeing as this role is fairly new, and most people won't have much experience performing it, what we need to look at is the qualities that the candidates possess, to try to find the optimal match for the needs of the project and product. To be very successful in the role, the product owner needs to have sufficient depth and breadth in their domain. Finding someone in house with both can be a challenge. Experience has shown that finding someone with the right set of attributes, and training them where they need it, is much better than finding someone with experience but lacking the essential skills.

Here are some of the skills a good product owner should possess:

Be able to craft and express the product vision. Both of these skills are important to the final success of the project. The product owner must be able to create the vision for the product, which includes the end state, as well all of the intermediate states along the way. They must also be able to effectively communicate this vision, in a way that all stakeholders can internalize. This means that they are able to create a product vision, put it together in a way that everyone from developers to executives can understand, and can then break down the vision into discrete chunks that can be delivered.

This vision needs to be described, constantly and consistently, to the project team, who then needs proper guidance and adjustments to deliver the proper result. The product owner must also act as a small business owner or entrepreneur, and create a culture of creativity and innovation, and be someone who is able to get the best work out of the team. As requirements and needs change, the market zigs and zags and the product morphs into something different than originally specified, it is the product owner's job to keep the team aligned, and to keep the stakeholders expectations on track. Without the ability to do both at the same time, the product will wind up disappointing one group or the other.

Be able to lead, follow, and play along. These are actually three different skills, and they rarely naturally occur all in the same person. It takes all three skills to do the job well, something that is both a strength and a weakness of an Agile organization.

A leader's role is to craft a vision, express it in way that excites and motivates, and drive the vision until it becomes reality. We have already discussed how this is one of the primary tasks of the product owner; only they have the full vision, and only they are the arbiter of whether or not the vision has been fulfilled or if more work is required to reach it. So it seems somewhat obvious to say that the product owner needs to be a good leader, at least in this respect.

The other two are less obvious, however. Why does a product owner need to be both a leader and a follower?

There's a saying that "none of us are smarter than all of us;"[1] being a product owner is no different. The person in the role needs to be ready to follow someone or something that might improve the product, no matter what the source of the idea was. The product owner cannot be the source of all power, and cannot dictate without listening. This isn't a license for the product owner to be weak, or expect others to do their job for them. What it means is that the product owner must be ready to actively follow, and adopt as their own, any idea that will have the result of improving the product. Being an active follower doesn't make you less of a leader; in fact it can enhance the position. And it's very important to understand the difference.

And that's why it is so vital to be a good team player; to learn to play along. Agile teams are meant to be made up of peers, smart people from many disciplines who are all working towards the same goal. But while all the team members are equal, some are more equal than others. When it comes to a final resolution, it's the product owner who makes the final call. This comes with some power and some responsibility that the other team members generally don't need to shoulder. Being sure to leverage the entire team's ability, gain consensus and achieve an optimal outcome is, when it comes down to it, the responsibility of the product owner. Leading, following and being a good team member are all parts of the job.

Be able and willing to communicate, over-communicate, and then communicate a little more. Most of the product owner's role is to communicate. They must talk with

---

[1] This quote is attributed to Kenneth Blanchard

customers, users, sponsors, executives, team members, supporters, detractors, developers, service people and management. Requirements need to be created and discussed, constraints and trade-offs need to be called out and clearly described, and compromise will be needed to make any progress, all of which require effective and constant communications.

Some view the product owner as the representative of the customer; others view them as the representative of the business. The product owner often views himself as a part of the development team as well as a sponsor of the project. In reality, the product owner is all these things, and none of these things. A good product owner has to refrain from "taking sides" in discussions. They can't be on the side of the developer or the customer, management or finance. They have to remain on the side of the product, and the product only, carefully balancing the needs of everyone, while maintaining the health of the product vision. And all of this takes communication.

Dedicated and trusted. A successful product owner needs to have the trust of all involved. Over the course of the project, they will make hundreds or thousands of decisions, and this must be done with the confidence of management, the team, and other stakeholders. A project that is fraught with frequent escalations, particularly if the product owner gets overturned, isn't set up to be successful. The role of product owner is to be the single voice directing the future of the product. Once the team starts to believe that there is more than one owner, or that there is an easy avenue to ignore the direction of the product owner, then the team will quickly go off track, and chaos will ensue.

But trust is a two-way street. In order for the product owner to gain the trust of the customer, of management, and of the team, he must show that he is dedicated to the project. This doesn't necessarily mean that this product is the only thing that he is working on, but it is important to show that the product owner is committed to the success of the product itself. Certainly, no product owner wants their product to fail, but it's possible to set up a scenario where the success of product isn't the product owner's top priority. They may have other products, or other priorities, or working on something else that conflicts. This needs to be avoided as much as possible; if the success of a product isn't the product owner's top priority, then you have chosen the wrong product owner.

Highly available. Being a product owner is a serious responsibility, and depending on the size of the product or the size of the team, can very well be a full-time gig. There are two main reasons why the product owner needs to be highly available to the product. First, if the product owner has many other duties, then their performance as product owner will slip. This is simple mathematics; the more time the product owner spends on other tasks, they less they are spending on the product. Since the job of Agile product owner is highly collaborative, whatever time is taken away from the product is time that the product will suffer for it.

Second, and more specifically, is the manner in which Agile projects get run. The product owner is an integral part of the team, attending meetings and retrospectives, answering questions and clearing obstacles, and making sure that the product vision is communicated, over and over again. The more time a product owner spends performing other duties, the more that the team is going to be left on their own. If the team can't get a response from the product owner in a timely fashion, it will begin to start guessing, or answering their own questions. Usually the team is aligned, and is correct enough, but not always. But even worse, if the team is conditioned that the product owner isn't going to answer requests for clarification, they might stop asking altogether. This will eventually cause drift between the vision for the product that the product owner has, and the product that is actually being built. Being available to make sure this doesn't happen is a key to success in the role.

Product Owner interactions with the team

Most flavors of Agile project management consider the product owner as a full member of the project team. That's a key designation, and one that sets Agile apart from other philosophies. The product owner is equally responsible for the successful delivery of a successful product as everyone else on the team. This means that the product owner needs to be highly collaborative with the team, and interact with it as a member, not as a customer or client. There is no "Us vs. Them" relationship for the product owner, as the product owner is part of the "Us." This means that the product owner must participate in the team formation and growth, and help form it into a high-performing team over time.

As with any team, the longer they are allowed to learn to work together, they better they will perform. Many organizations will go to great lengths to keep their high-performing development teams together for as long as possible, even moving them as a unit from project to project. In an Agile team, there are two additional considerations for relationships to preserve, the product owner and the product itself. The longer a team works with the same product owner, the more they will understand how each other like to work, like to be communicated with, and what they value. Even though the product owner is filling a much different role than the developers, they are a vital part of the team, and changing out the product owner will lead to the team having to learn many things anew. The relationship of the team to the product itself also shouldn't be overlooked. Developers learn how to work with a product over time, understanding its strengths and weaknesses, and how it can be adapted and how it can't. And it is the product owner who helps bridge this gap, and helps the developers learn the product and fill in necessary details as needed.

Many flavors of Agile discuss the need for the project owner to sit with the team at all times. In fact, some of what you read will go so far as to actually require it, claiming that the project cannot succeed unless it happens. I find this to be hyperbole, no project is guaranteed success due to colocation, and no project is doomed to failure without it. However there is a good reason why this point is stressed. The product owner, ScrumMaster and development team need to work closely together and remain constantly in synch with each other. Today's reality will often put collocating teams out of reach. Even if your development team might not be on the other side of the world, it might be a short plane ride away. It may also be that your customers are on one coast, while your team is on another. Or maybe there's just no room for you to move in. There are many ways for you to keep in touch, and the tools are getting better and better for collaborative online spaces, video chat, secure document sharing, and more. However, the easiest way keep in touch with the team is by being near each other, sharing space, and even sharing a team room.

There are many values to having a team room assigned to your team. Not only is a room that you know is always available to you, it helps put the team in the right frame of mind for working and collaborating. It is also a place to store permanent artifacts, like the backlog listing, product visions and statements, and other things that the team should be constantly reminded about. Surely, many of these things can be achieved without dedicating a room to the team, but similar to collocating, having a team room makes it a lot easier. A team room has the added benefit for a product owner who cannot move in with the team – it becomes a place to go to be with the team while visiting, and a consistent place to connect with for discussions and collaborating.

Product Owner interactions with the project manager

Different versions of Agile use different terms for what historically was known as a project manager. Some of them use different words or have a different organization to make sure things are progressing the right way, such as ScrumMaster, Agile coach, or some other title. I'm going to break with regular Agile vocabulary by using the term project manager, only because there is no term for this role that covers all of Agile. However, all teams need someone who is guiding, coordinating and ensuring that the goals are indeed being met. No matter what that person is called, open collaboration with that person will be critical to the success of the product, and thus, the success of the product owner. Some of the Agile literature breaks it down this way: the product owner is responsible for deciding "what" to build, the project manager is responsible for "how" it is built. This means being responsible for the health of the team, that commitments are being met, that the team remains motivated, and that the level of quality remains high.

The project manager role is not meant to be adversarial from the product owner, it is meant to be a balance. It is very difficult for one person to play both roles on the same product at the same time, and can have the effect of setting up conflicts when considering the "how" vs. the "what." Virtually all advice is to not have the product owner be the same person as the project manager, and this is for good reason. Not only are both full time jobs, but they truly are different jobs with different goals, and trying to perform well in both is nearly impossible. With that in mind, the product owner should build a strong relationship with the person in the role, so that the balance works properly, and the vision and needs of the product continue to be met.

Product Owner interactions with other Stakeholders

There have been plenty of products that were executed properly, but turned into commercial failures because no one bought it. Even though the team might feel the project was a success, the market considers it a failure, and therefore, so should the product owner. Management, the product sponsor or steering committee, might feel differently. They might feel that all the right decisions were made, and an excellent product was produced, but there is some other reason that the product failed in the market. With all these stakeholders, all with different definitions of success, how is the product owner expected to navigate the path to success? The Agile answer is to get constant and frequent feedback, and to incorporate that feedback into the product as quickly as possible.

Usually, the point person for feedback from all stakeholders is the role of the product owner. These stakeholders include management, customers, the technical teams, users and support. It would take phenomenal genius, and an unlikely stroke of brilliant luck, to build exactly what all these stakeholders want just going on one person's intuition. This is exactly why Agile has a feedback loop built into its foundation; the product owner should take advantage of it. Shipping a new version or a new release, asking for feedback from all sides, and then adjusting and shipping again is exactly the process that Agile espouses. Since you have multiple stakeholders, with someone conflicting, if not competing, goals and desires, using frequent inspect and adapt cycles allows the project to see the outcome that maximizes the return for all of them. Reaching this maximum is the product owners responsibility.

Handling very large products

Agile works perfectly when the size of the product is small enough for one person to understand all the implications and interactions, and personally manage and decide the direction the product should take, even at the detail level. Because of this, there is some wisdom in sizing your products and projects to the size that one person can handle. The methodology is targeted at starting as small as possible, and only adding to is slowly, and as the team can handle it. As the team gets more experienced, it can handle more and more complexity, and work with an increasingly expanding product. Beginning with a team that is too large, or attempting to build too much, can cause enough difficulty that it can remove a lot of the flexibility and agility that the methodology requires.

It isn't always possible to start small and to grow organically. Some products by their nature have to start out large, such as building an entire airport, and some products have been around for years or decades, and have complexity already built in from the start. The way that Agile scales is to continue to break the work down into team-sized streams, until one person can handle all of it. These would make up a team-of-teams, or in Scrum, a Scrum-of-Scrums. Scaling this way allows the methodology to still be used as intended, while allowing for bigger things to get accomplished. This is done by creating new roles; for the product owner role, it creates the need for a Chief Product Owner.

Rather than having a very large project, Agile recommends creating many smaller teams, and aggregating them together into one larger effort. Every team needs a single product owner, and a product owner can only manage a few teams. Depending on the size, complexity, difficulty and experience of the product owner, it's likely they can only manage one team effectively, but even the best product owner will probably max out at two teams. Beyond two, the product owner starts to lose focus, and will eventually be caught between the teams, and not be able to effectively lead any of them.

This creates a situation where more than two product owners are required in order to bring a product to market. This seems to be a contradiction; the methodology works best when there is one and only one product owner, but to properly deliver the product, we need multiple product owners. The solution is somewhat simple, and continues to align with the Agile goals. The solution is to have one person responsible for the for the vision of the entire product, and to have other people responsible for delivering on the pieces of the vision. This means that a large product can have several product owners, but only one Chief Product Owner.

The role of the Chief Product Owner is to lead the other product owners, ensure that the vision is consistently communicated, and optimize delivery among all the teams. This means working to create a product-wide understanding and consensus, while also having the final voting rights if no agreement can be reached. Sometimes, the CPO also acts as a product owner on a piece of the product; this is especially true if the product grew on its own, and more product owners were added. However, it's not impossible for the CPO to not act as a product owner themselves; rather they guide the rest of the product owners into reaching the vision.

Note that the skills to be a good Chief Product Owner are similar, but slightly different than those that make a good Product Owner. Rather than dealing with development teams, you are dealing with other product owners. Instead of being responsible for creating a well prioritized and groomed backlog, your primary concern is ensuring that all the product owners understand the vision for the product, and are acting appropriately. The CPO is often more responsible for dealing with executives and high-level customers, and balancing the goals of the teams to deliver the value the customers require, rather than trying to maximize the value of a single team. The good news is that the CPO role is an excellent construct for delivering a large product, and it's also a reasonable career path for someone who has been a product owner.

Because of this, determining who should be appointed product owner is a challenge. The role is so vital to the success of the product that having the right person on the team is important even for a small product. For a large product, it becomes even more important, as the person who becomes a product owner probably has an eye to becoming a chief product owner. In general there are two ways to organize a team of this size, and how you organize will help decide who the right person for each role may be.

If you are faced with creating a team of teams, there are two main patterns to follow. The first pattern is to have each team be fully autonomous, owning their own space, including all the business, technical and customer requirements for their area. This is the traditional product management role, and isn't much different than staffing a single team. Each of the product owners own their own domain, and need all the regular skills that a product owner should have as we discussed earlier in this chapter. The chief product owner should be similar, as their goal is to continually express the vision, and motivate the teams to deliver against the vision. The teams will be looking to the CPO for final decisions, but for the most part, each team is on its own, and just need to be monitored for vision and direction, and not for any other facet of their role.

The second pattern is to have some teams dependent on other teams. For instance, if the product is made up of five teams, two of them can be infrastructure and service teams, while the other three are creating the business components and customer-facing features. This is actually not a best practice, as it means that none of the teams have a single point of decision, and the priorities are being set by someone outside of their team. However, sometimes this is the only option available based on the personnel on hand, or the problem the teams face. When this happens, the CPO tends to play much less of a customer-facing role, and much more of an architectural and foundational role. If you are faced with this scenario, the product owners tend to be more like traditional product owners, while the teams that the other teams are depending upon tend to be more technical architects. The CPO in this setup usually is a blend of both, but it's not uncommon for them to be more technical than customer-focused.

Whichever organization your product needs, there are solutions that work for both. History has shown that the more you make the teams dependent on each other, the less agile you will become. But if the hand you are dealt requires it, it's still possible to succeed. Just be sure that everyone knows what their role is, and what they are trying to accomplish. And no matter which way you head, note the consistent and constant communication is the key to everything.

Anti-Patterns in Product Ownership

The concept of anti-patterns is one of my favorites. My definition of an anti-pattern is a solution to a common problem that many organizations implement, but one that rarely or never works. For more information about Anti-patterns, simply search online or on Amazon, you will find several books on the topic, all of which are a perfect combination of hilarious, depressing and spot-on true to life.

Moving to product ownership is a challenge, and fraught with difficulties, traps and tricks. Each of them seems reasonable to a point, but if you are faced with the actual situation, or if you dig one or two levels deeper, you'll see that the arrangement could never have worked. While I think we are all comfortable with asking people to be flexible or stretch muscles that they haven't used before, it is our obligation to make sure that they are doing so in a way that could possibly succeed.

The neutered product owner. I could also call this the "let's wait-and-see" product owner. It's highly unlikely that an organization has a stable of well-trained, highly skilled people on staff just waiting to be product owners. It's a newer role, and there are probably several people who are viewed as partially qualified, or people who management thinks they have the skill, but they aren't entirely certain. So, management does something that seems reasonable, but in the end, winds up damaging everyone involved: they appoint a product owner, and decide that they will give them authority, but they will watch them closely. This actually seems like a good outcome; it gives someone an opportunity, while allowing management the comfort that someone is double-checking their work and ensuring that things are going in the right direction. In fact, this winds up damaging the employee, the product, and the Agile effort in general.

What this anti-pattern actually does is put an un-empowered product owner in a role where they must be empowered. If the development teams discovers that all of the product owner's decisions are being double checked or second-guessed, then they will learn that they don't need to listen to the product owner in the first place. If the product owner feels compelled to check with their manager or steering committee for all but the most basic decisions, then the development team will begin consulting these people directly. This will cause the team to lose confidence in the product owner and quite likely the product itself. If the product owner is put in a position where they are nominally in charge, but are neutered in reality, then everyone is set up to fail.

The low-bandwidth product owner. Since we have established that there probably aren't that many people on staff who are ready to be product owners, another idea is to overburden an existing product owner. The idea is that even an overworked, but experienced product owner is better than a rookie or someone who doesn't know what they are doing. The hope is that getting someone with experience for 10-20% of their time is much better than getting a novice who is 100% dedicated to the task. This is another case where the idea sounds good, but in practice, all it winds up doing a lot more harm than good.

A product owner who doesn't have the right amount of time to dedicate to the task starts getting behind on what Steven Covey called "Quadrant II" tasks – important but not urgent. The backlog starts to get messy and less groomed, planning and retrospective meetings start to get missed. Eventually, the product owner starts delaying responses to critical project questions. One of the tenets of Agile development is to promote a sustainable process and to create a pace that can be continued indefinitely. Overburdening a product owner, or having one that misses meetings or neglects basic duties isn't sustainable. This situation should be avoided if at all possible.

There are two general flavors of the no-bandwidth product owner. The first is when the product owner isn't afforded the time to properly perform the role, and thus, certain important tasks get skipped or missed entirely. Some organizations don't realize how much time it takes to properly perform the product owner role, and thus they assign it as an additional duty to someone's already busy schedule. No matter how skilled or well-intentioned the product owner is, there simply isn't enough time in their day to do the job well. Critical tasks lapse, and the team winds up being ineffective. This probably isn't a sign of poor performance; if the product owner had the bandwidth, the team could have been high-performing. But based on the product owner's availability, it wasn't to be.

The second kind of no-bandwidth product owner comes from within. Sometimes the team itself misunderstands the role, and collaborates and makes decisions without the product owner's knowledge or input. This dynamic winds up putting the product owner perpetually playing catch-up, so they have to work extra hard simply to stay two steps behind. The product owner is available, but all their bandwidth is consumed trying to keep up with a team that is racing ahead. This invariably becomes a bad situation for all involved. Eventually, the team will stop including them entirely, as they are so far behind that they can't add value to the team or product.

The two-headed product owner. The product owner is intended to own all facets of the product, from determining the feature set, to how it will be marketed, and even how it is released and serviced. It's highly unlikely that there is someone that is personally knowledgeable in all these areas on staff, and even less likely that the organization has several of these people laying around. Because of this, companies hit upon the idea of splitting the role between two or more people, appointing someone to manage the more technical details, while someone else handles the traditional marketing aspects of the product. This seems like a great idea; put someone who knows each domain in charge, and all the right decisions will be made. Not only does this rarely work, this is actually counter to Agile at its core.

Splitting the role brings us back to the "us vs. them" scenario, where you are setting up the technical product owner to be at odds with the marketing product owner. If you look at this idea close enough, it probably looks very much like whatever organization you currently have. Additionally, by putting more than one person in a role of responsibility and accountability, you wind up having no one who is accountable. The product owner is meant to do whatever is right for the *product*; this scenario will have product owners with conflicting priorities, who will eventually fight for whatever is right for their *function*.

Note that this is different than creating two separate teams, and using a CPO over them both to make sure that resourcing and prioritization are correct between them. This is having more than one product owner with only one team. While it does sound like a good idea, it's actually a bad one, and misses a lot of the point of the role in the first place.

The vice-product owner. Sometimes, the ideal product owner is unable to logistically perform the duties. Perhaps they are already overburdened (see above) or perhaps they are located in another office or another country. Perhaps they work remotely, or they spend a large percentage of their time travelling. This is often solved with a fairly simple statement, "When I'm not around, Mary is in charge. Treat her like you'd treat me." We see this pattern in many instances, including the President of the United States. There's a false hope that Mary will be the same, in every way, as the original product owner.

This anti-pattern has the same problems as the two-headed product owner described above. Communication suffers, misunderstandings occur, decisions tend to need to be made and remade (and sometimes unmade) and sometimes the vice-product owner doesn't feel comfortable making certain decisions, and thus holds up the team while they try to find the real product owner on the road. The best-case result is a team that isn't very agile, they need to wait for final decisions to be made. The worst-case is a dysfunctional team that is fraught with poor communication and hurt feelings.

Separately from the two-headed product owner, where the anti-pattern is used to fill a gap in skills, the gap here tends to be availability or even location. It's possible that the product owner you have chosen shouldn't have been selected, someone closer to the development team, or with more time, should have been chosen, instead. Or perhaps the development team needs to be moved, or a new product owner hired and brought on board. All of these solutions are better than the having someone other than the product owner in charge.

The Role of a Product Owner

By now you have probably noticed a theme. The key to Agile success requires accountability, in the form of a single person, and open and frequent collaboration with everyone involved in the product. Gone are the days of the product manager writing a requirements document that is hundreds of pages long, then turning that over to a business analyst to specify out the details, who then turns the specification document over to a project manger to execute and deliver.

The product owner is meant to be a full and integral part of the team, and not treated as a client who must be pleased, or an adversary that must be competed against. In fact, in some of the earliest versions of some Agile methods, there was no role for a ScrumMaster, Agile coach or project manager. While this did prove to be unworkable, the intent was to put the product owner as close to the team as possible.

Close collaboration, accountability and clear and decisive communications are the keys to Agile success. And they are all the job of the Product Owner.

Chapter 2

Creating the Product Vision

Some of the most successful and revolutionary products ever created have a clear and energizing vision. These visions are even compelling enough to become marketing slogans, such as "1,000 songs in your pocket" or "Yeah, we've got that." It turns out that creating a clear and compelling vision is even more important internally than it is externally. Once the product exists, the market can view it, inspect it, hold it, and decide for itself if it has value. The vision may help sell the product, but in the end, it's the product that sells.

Internally, however, the product doesn't exist yet. There is nothing to hold, nothing to play with. Your team needs to picture it in their heads, and see how it could be used and what value it would provide. And they need to do this in the face of changing priorities, initial feedback from customers, and other things that are going to weigh them down. This makes the vision critical not only for the success of the product, but even to the completion of the product in the first place.

The Vision

We've already mentioned Steven Covey once already, but another of his "7 Habits" is the idea of starting with the end in mind. That is, if you don't know what you are doing, you have no idea if you are doing it right, nor do you even know when you are done. The vision is meant to be an image of the final product, so that you can compare what you have against that vision and mark progress, or even decide if the product is ready to ship.

Traditional products would often have documents such as a charter, or a scope document, or something like a statement of what the team was doing and what they weren't. Having these artifacts was certainly better than not having them, but they pre-supposed something that Agile disagrees exists: a notion of specifically what the market wants *before* putting something into the market.

The vision is meant to align everyone working on the product. They can view themselves using the product, even if they can't actually see the product themselves. The vision for the iPod of "1,000 songs in your pocket" is more meaningful than "A 3x5 inch block of plastic that also is a music player." The first description describes the product's usefulness and the utility that it provides to the customer. The second describes what the product is, without any real view into how or why the customer's life would be improved for owning it.

Some products have universal appeal; nearly everyone listens to music. Most of us aren't as lucky, and are working on a product for a specific segment of the population. Even more, most of the people on the team won't be in that segment, so they will need to understand what the customer, what their needs are, and how this product will solve some of those needs.

What the Vision Should Include

The vision should cover a lot of ground in as few words as possible. It would be great if it could be done in five words, but that's not the norm. But ideally the vision could be kept to 100 words or less, while still giving enough of a picture to the listener to formulate their own thoughts about the product. Let's look at the topics that the vision should strive to cover.

The customers. The vision should have an idea for who the customers for the product are. Are they going to be buying it themselves, or buying it for others to use? How many customers do we envision having, and how many users? What do these people value; are they most interested in price, power, or design? How sensitive to quality are they? What won't they value?

The need. Now the we understand the customer, we next need to understand what their needs are. Ideally it will be a need that they are willing to pay to solve. Then we need to gain an understanding of how the product will solve that need, and how that solution is better than whatever the customer is already doing. If this is an unsolved need, then perhaps all we need to do is create a working product. But if this is meant to be a better solution than anything that exists currently, we need to make sure that our product is indeed better than anything on the market.

The highlights. We need to understand what the product must do in order for it to be compelling. For instance, "Small enough to fit in your pocket" is implied in the iPod vision; if it was too big, it wouldn't be a success. What are the selling points that will get the market excited and differentiate it from anything else currently available? It should contain something about what the product will do, and what the product will do better than anyone else. Many great products have one or two great features, causing customers to overlook that the rest of it is standard. Calling those out as part of the vision will help people understand.

The existing market. Sometimes, we are solving a need that no one else has yet. More often, we are making a product that is intended to be a big improvement. The team should be able to envision what the customer is already using, and why they would switch. Knowing what the customer's existing pain points and frustrations are with the existing products is important to making a product that delights. Understanding the market will help round out the vision for the environment the product is attempting to enter.

The business. Finally, the vision should have a small amount of information about the business itself. Even if the product is obviously valuable and needed, a description of how it can be made profitably will help set the product in the framework of the company. Knowing the business model will also help guide the release plan, and how the product will be monetized. Knowing how it will be made, sold and supported will also help determine what direction the product takes during development. Some will argue that the needs of the business should never come ahead of the needs of the product, and those people are generally right. But to not at least understand the needs of the business isn't excusable.\

If the product being launched is part of an entirely new product line, or a new business, then putting it context will help. This could be the first product of several, so including a small mention of the entire strategy might be helpful. If this is an addition to an existing line, showing how it will enhance the line and interact with the other products will also help people understand where it fits in the overall strategy. The fuller the picture you can give, the better the vision will add value to the product itself.

Attributes of a Good Vision

We just went through what kinds of things should compose the vision. Not every vision is going to contain each topic, of course, and some of the things will just be hinted at. The goal isn't to create a vision that will exactly describe the entire product and market to someone who has little background or context at all. Rather, the vision is for the team and the people who do know enough about the idea that the vision cements the idea in their head. Let's look at some of the enduring qualities that we would like our vision to possess.

One vision per product. There should be only one vision for the product; everyone on the team should have the same vision. There shouldn't be a concept of a technical vision, or a marketing vision, a manufacturing vision or a service vision. There should be one vision that everyone shares, and everyone is striving towards. Having multiple visions is simply another way to fracture your team. The technical team may say that they have achieved their vision, even if another group has not. Or worse, one team might strive to reach their vision in a way that prevents another team from reaching theirs. This is a bad situation for all involved.

In order to be helpful, a vision needs to help unite everyone who is working on the product into one shared picture of the future. In this way, everyone on the team, no matter the function or role, is driving to the same outcome. Creating and maintaining a shared vision is one of the most difficult and most important tasks that a product owner faces.

Inspiring and flexible. The main purpose of a vision is to align and inspire the team. Most of your team will want to feel a sense of pride and ownership about the product they are developing, no matter what industry or domain you are in. It's rare that focusing on the business aspect of the product will inspire the team; few authors set out to write best-sellers, they set out to write a novel that people will read and enjoy. The same is true for your product; unless you are creating a printing press, if the vision includes "make a lot of money," then your vision will probably fail to properly motivate and inspire the team.

In addition, it must also be flexible enough to allow the team to mold the vision into something that inspires them, as well as providing for the creativity of the collective team to make the vision even better. Previously, we discussed the idea of a product owner as a follower. If the product vision is too rigid, then there is hardly any avenue by which the development team can help improve it. It is also important to leave room open for the customers and the market to guide the direction of the product, as feedback is solicited and generated. Thinking that we know all about the product before the product even exists is generally not a good idea.

It's also important not to specify features or to go into too much detail when creating the product vision. The vision isn't meant to be a specification, it's meant to be a fairly short, but inspiring statement that helps guide the team towards the right direction, while leaving room for them to find a better way there. The more you strictly specify up front, the more you lose the gains that come from the feedback loops inherent in the Agile methodology.

Brief and memorable. Some have described the product vision as the elevator pitch. If you were only given two minutes or less to describe your product, what would you say about it? In many ways, the less you say, the better. The vision should be easily memorable, with between one and three highlights that stick with the listener for a long time. It is relatively easy, and much more comfortable, to come up with a list of features, or a list of things that the product will do. It's much harder to express why the product is different, or why customers should buy it. The clearer the value proposition of the product is, the more likely someone is to buy it, support it, or fund it.

It's important to note that your team will be repeating the vision to their friends, co-workers and colleagues. And, much like the child's game of telephone, they will forget certain aspects, and get some of it wrong. Therefore, the more complicated the vision is, the more wrong they will be when they start spreading the vision to others. The easier the vision is to understand, internalize and repeat to others, the more likely the vision of the product is to spread and grow.

The Minimal Viable Product (MVP)

There is a funny commercial on television where befuddled investors ask for a pair of "foresight goggles." The man behind the counter lets the investor know that the foresight goggles have been discontinued, due to them fogging up a lot. This is a pretty close analog to the market for most products; there is simply no way for us to know in advance if the product that we are building is one that people will buy, let alone be excited about. And yet, most traditional project and product management methodologies espouse doing a lot of upfront research, perhaps for several years, and then attempting to release a product fully formed and market-ready all at once. I suspect you can count the number of "v1" products that were a huge success and were never upgraded on one hand. Or possibly none.

One of the tenets of Agile is to launch early and often. No amount of research or analysis will tell you what product the market wants and is willing to pay for; only the market will tell you that. In fact, there is a high likelihood that research and analysis will actually lead you astray. Therefore, you must launch your product and get feedback before you can figure out what the optimal offering might be. Many popular products were launched as infants, without key features, and were upgraded over time. The first iPad didn't have a camera, and the first iPod was actually combined with a Motorola RAZR (the ROXR) to everyone's dismay. No one really recalls these products, even five years later; people know what the products are now, not what they used to be.

Agile has a name for this kind of process, called the Minimal Viable Product, or more aptly named, MVP. The MVP is a version of the product that has the minimal feature set and attributes that would cause anyone to buy it at all. For instance, an iPod that doesn't actually play music would fail to be viable. But the same player that doesn't have advanced playlist creation or infrared synching far exceeds MVP status. Determining when viability has been reached is another key responsibility of the product owner.

This thinking is counter to what most product management courses would teach. In order to make an impact on the market, you need to have an impactful product. For instance, trying to launch a new automobile that doesn't have a radio or power windows sounds like a failure from the start. But launching software or a website that has only 20% of the intended features might actually get you closer to success than waiting.

The product owner must determine the minimal feature set and capabilities of the product that will engage the customer. Engaging the customer is the goal; you want them to take the product, touch it and play with it. But most of all, you want them to complain about it. You want the customers to start telling you what features are missing, and what they want most of all. You might even get some comments on features that are useless and could be safely abandoned. If your product is too under-capable, then the customer will just ignore it, if it's too feature-rich, then you will be too invested in ideas that haven't been tested yet. Like all things Agile, it's a delicate balance.

We have determined that knowing for certain what is going to delight the market isn't possible without actually engaging the market; releasing is the best path to launching a remarkable product. This is especially true in industries where launching a new version is extremely cheap, like software or a website. But it's also true for physical products that have to be manufactured and shipped. For instance, in the first 31 months of Apple's iPad release, there were eight versions created and shipped.[2] Many companies and product owners are afraid of launching the wrong product, so they will hold up the release until they are comfortable with what they are sending into the market. Agile disagrees.

As a product owner, you should *never* be fully comfortable with what you have produced until the market gets to have its say. There is a bit of a tightrope walker attitude needed to do this properly. You know you are headed in the right direction, but you aren't positive that your plan to get there is going to work. The only way to know for sure is to start walking, and adjust your balance along the way.

There are a few other advantages of launching an MVP. First, if you are selling a product, then you will start to generate some revenue. Even if sales are disappointing, they are still better than no sales at all. And as soon as a product has paying customers, the game changes for everyone

---

[2] iPad 1 (April 3, 2010) , iPad 1 w/3G (April 30, 2010) , iPad 2 (March 11, 2011) , iPad 3 (March 16, 2012) , iPad 4 (November 2, 2012) , iPad mini (November 2, 2012) , iPad Air (November 1, 2013) , iPad mini 2 (November 12, 2013)

involved. Second, it's possible that your product missed the mark completely. Maybe no one really wanted your Wi-Fi enabled umbrella. If that's the case, you'll find out pretty quickly once you try to sell it. If you can't sell a single one, then you can save a lot of time, money and headache by cutting the product short, and moving onto something else.

This doesn't mean that you should launch and sit idle, while you wait for comments to roll in. Your product should have a release plan that covers present and future releases, to give a direction to the team. While the product is getting released and is still in its infancy, the next revision can be being worked on and getting prepped for a follow-on launch. However, the product owner must be listening for feedback from customers, and be ready to adjust the plan as it comes in. If customers are nearly unanimous about the need for a certain thing, then that should be prioritized highly on the backlog, and perhaps scheduled for the next release if possible.

It is okay for the product owner to have guessed wrong about what customers would value. In fact, it's expected. But what is not okay is to not react when the customers start telling you what is missing or what should change. It is exactly this adaptability that separates Agile from other methodologies. And launching your MVP is the most reliable way to get the information you need.

The Importance of Focus

It's almost trite these days to talk about focus, and how without it, your project will fail. Lots of management, self-help and productivity books all praise the concept of focusing on what is important, and ignoring all else. But when it comes to a product vision, the value of focus cannot be overlooked. Your team and your customers want to know how your product is better than what already exists, or how it solves their problem in a unique and compelling manner. Without this, few people will even pay attention to your product, let alone provide you feedback on it.

Be as simple as possible, but no simpler.[3] Simplicity is often misunderstood, and sometimes abused. Simplicity sometimes is misconstrued as a license to be vague or to not be diligent in certain aspects of the vision. In reality, that's exactly the opposite of what this tenet states.

A vision should be simple enough to be instantly understood, and should focus on what differentiates the product in the market or in people's lives. A vision that lists out dozens of features or use cases isn't going to work; for a vision to be compelling it needs to be distilled down to the primary use and the primary value. Swiss army knives are well known for their versatility, but rarely does anyone say "If only I had a Swiss army knife!" Rather, they lament not having a ¼" hacksaw, or a corkscrew, or some other function. While it's true that the Swiss knife would have these features, note that no one is asking for it specifically.

That's the bar you are trying to reach. You want people to understand what your product excels at, what it does and doesn't do, and know when to be asking for your product specifically. If you can't craft a story around where your product is truly superlative, then you haven't crafted a good

---

[3] This quote is attributed to Albert Einstein

enough vision. While there certainly is a business model around being second or third best at several tasks, it's not something that products should strive to achieve. Being the best at one thing is generally better than being second best at five things.

You are not your khakis[4]. One of the fallacies of product ownership is to create a product that has more features than anyone else. If you competition does 12 things and you do 15, then your product must be superior. This is a comforting theory, but it's completely wrong. For instance, I have one of those bottle opener/corkscrew/pop-top gadgets in my kitchen. I never use it. When I need to open a bottle of wine, I use my wine opener. When I need to open a bottle of beer, I use my best bottle opener. Do you see the picture? Merely *having* the features isn't enough, you need to actually be best (or nearly best) at them in order for them to matter.

The Agile Manifesto[5] includes the following principle: "the art of maximizing the amount of work not done--is essential." When we apply this to the creation of the product vision, we can see that the art of not over-including features and functionality into the vision is critical to success. Your vision should focus on what the product does well, and make no mention of things that it does poorly, or not at all. Since you have left your product vision flexible enough to react to the needs of the team, if a feature is needed, the team will let you know. If a feature isn't needed, then the team will let you know that, as well.

---

[4] I dropped a word out of this quote from Fight Club.
[5] http://agilemanifesto.org/principles.html

Make certain that your vision is clean and uncluttered, and focuses specifically on where it will differentiate from other products in the market. It will be these differentiators that will determine success or failure of your product.

Focus on the Customer

As much as this sounds like a line from the movie Office Space, focusing on the customer is the essence of the product vision. Choosing which customer need the product is meant to solve is both difficult and critical to the success of the product in general. This can be a difficult nuance to understand. There are things that the product does, and there are problems that the product addresses. Certainly there is overlap between the two, but they aren't the same thing. Understanding what problems your product is attempting to address is even more important than understanding what features it possesses.

This is why focusing on the customer point of view is so helpful. I can't source the quote appropriately, but there is a line that states that no customer wants a ¼" drill, what they want is a ¼" hole. Focusing on what the customer wants will lead you to a different direction than focusing on what the product can do. From the customer point of view, they know what they want and need. If you are busy focusing on what the product can do, you are paying attention to the wrong thing.

Parts of the Product Vision

There are two separate parts to our product vision, what the product must do, and what the product must be. The former is based on what the customer needs, and how the product meets those needs. For instance, I need my cell phone to be able to ring when someone calls. Without this, the phone is useless. Different Agile methodologies call these needs "use cases" or "user stories" or something similar, to get an understanding of what the customer is trying to do with the product.

On the other side is what the product must be -- form, rather than function. These can be things such as size, cost, elegance of design or ease of use. They are the things that differentiate similar products from each other; if both products meet the same need, then the customer is likely to choose the one that most meets their vision for what the product is like.

It turns out, it's this second list that is more important to provide guidance to the team. This list becomes the set of constraints that they must work under while designing solutions that meet the customer's user needs. For instance, if the product vision includes a $99 price point, then the team knows it can't include any very expensive components. Or if the idea is to keep the product in your handbag or pocket, then you know that it can't get too hot while in operation.

These two lists combined make up the core of the environment in which your team will work. Expressing both the needs of the customer, and the qualities of the product, we are now starting to link the technical solution with the finished product itself. A technical solution that meets the requirements, but doesn't solve the customer needs is a useless product. Similarly, something that solves the customer's needs, but is unworkable due to a flaw in its form is unlikely to sell or be properly maintained.

Just like user stories need to be prioritized, so too do the product qualities. This is especially important when the desired qualities come into conflict. For instance, if we have a desire to have a small product, as well as keeping the price point low, we might run into a conflict if the smaller components are also the most expensive ones. The result of this kind of conflict is a healthy tension, and it is this kind of tension that is the product owner's responsibility to break.

There are many books on how to prioritize lists of requirements, so I won't go too deeply here. In general, they all have a similar framework. Some call it "must have, should have, nice to have" others will call it "As, Bs and Cs." Whatever your team calls it, the idea is that there are requirements that the product must have (As), requirements that it should have (Bs) and those that can sacrificed in order to get more As or Bs in (Cs.) In fact, one of the best practices to determine the type of requirement you are given is to ask the question "If, in order get requirement X into the product, I have to not do requirement Y at all, is that okay?" The flip side is "Doing requirement Y will prevent us from doing X, is that okay?" This kind of pairwise decision making helps bring much clarity to the discussion.

Whatever process you use, you need to have a blend of customer needs and qualities of the product itself. They must work hand-in-hand, and inform each other along the way. In the past, a product manager would express the need, and allow the team to determine how best to solve it. In Agile, the product owner is a part of the team, and needs to be involved in all facets of the product development, including helping make tradeoff decisions that impact the product.

Visioning

While the vision for a product is being constructed, there are lots of stories and thoughts, hopes and dreams about what the product will eventually wind up being. A colleague of mine used to call this the "Santa Claus" factor. Everyone involved is certain that the vision will be delivering just the right present for them. Of course, this never turns out to be the case. We discussed above about the need for a simple vision, the product cannot be all things to all people. But in this stage of the vision, people are still hopeful that it will be.

This scenario can continue even while the product is being constructed. The first vision is generally directionally correct, but lacking many specifics. This is actually intentionally done in Agile methodologies, having too sharp of a vision too early on will suppress creativity and innovation, and will prevent the team from incorporating customer feedback the way that it should. The process requires you to ship the product as early as possible, get comments from the marketplace, and adapt as you go.

In general, there are two ways that product visions get created. They can either spring from a single, passionate individual, or they can be created by the development team. Both have advantages and disadvantages, and you don't always get to choose when and where inspiration will strike. But it is important to understand the difference.

The passionate individual vision. Depending on the company, it's possible for someone to come up with an idea on their own, get the idea approved and see it through to delivery. Some companies even view this as a best practice, allowing their employees to be innovative around whatever strikes their fancy will lead to a good outcome. The history is mixed, while plenty of outstanding, innovative and successful products have been conceived this way, there are many more that weren't successful, or the team could never actually get on board with the vision, causing disappointing results.

You may find yourself in the position of owning a product that was wholly conceived by one person. It's even possible that the person is you, but that isn't always the case. Sometimes, the person who comes up with the idea isn't the right person to be a product owner, so you'll inherit it. Other times, the single-thinker will be an executive, or someone who has the will to get the product started, but not the skill to keep it going.

If you do find yourself in this position, there are a few things that you must do in order to succeed. The value of a vision increases as it gets shared. The more people who understand and are aligned with the idea, the more power it has as a way to guide people towards the same goal. In this situation, the project begins with only one person understanding the vision. Your first task is to change that.

One of the primary tenets of Agile is equality, and being on the same team. If you are the only one who understands the vision, then you have set up an unequal relationship with the team, which will quickly devolve into the "us vs. them" scenario that we are trying to avoid. There is too much risk that you will start thinking to yourself, "I know exactly what this product needs, I just need a team to build it." While many great products were built this way, they weren't build using Agile.

In addition to making sure your vision is understood by everyone, you must also allow the team to alter the product to better fit the team. This can be difficult; someone had an idea that was fully-formed, and now the agile team is going to be given the chance to change it. As we discussed earlier, the collective experience of your team is one of the bigger assets your product has, you need to use them to their fullest.

Equally importantly, however, is the need for your product to be successfully constructed. In order for an Agile project team to produce a good outcome, they must be aligned and they must have the goals firmly set into their minds. The best way to do this is to allow the team to mold and shape the idea in a way that allows them to adopt the vision as their own. Once the team views the product as something of their own creation, then you have a good chance of creating a high-performing team. And that's one of the key ingredients you'll need to achieve.

The team-constructed vision. Often, your team will be assembled and work will begin before the vision is fully constructed. Either you, as product owner, haven't had the time to give the product enough thought, or you simply have certain aspects of the product undecided. This isn't a bad situation to be in, as it allows you to avoid some of the pitfalls of the single-person vision above, as well as use Agile to help you construct it.

Starting from scratch allows the team to be fully engaged and involved in the creation of the vision, and allows them to be fully invested in seeing it come to fruition. There are few things more valuable to a product owner than a fully engaged and invested team. But more than that, it allows you to use the methodology to create the vision, giving the team time to get to know each other, and for you to get to know them.

Agile has a concept of a "backlog" which is basically the list of things to do next. Nowhere in the definition of a backlog item is that it must be software or something constructed. All it states is that it is something for the team to work on. With that in mind, using the backlog to help create the vision is not only a perfectly valid thing to do; it's actually a great way to use the team.

The backlog tracker can contain visioning items, such as holding focus groups with prospective customers, doing competitive analysis, or sketching out color schemes or user interface designs on the whiteboard. It can also contain prototyping activities, such as creating working UI designs, or mocking up demos for customers to play with. The results of all these activities will help inform the vision, and the team will have been involved at every step.

There are advantages to having a full-formed vision before the product team begins work, and there are different advantages to having the team discover the vision as it moves along. No matter the situation you are in, you can create a great product, as long as you recognize the situation and act in an inclusive manner. That is the secret sauce of Agile, and it is okay to use the process for everything. In fact, it's highly encouraged.

Vision Creation

Up till now, we have been fairly theoretical when it comes to the product vision. We know we must have one, and we know that the team needs to be invested in it. If we don't have one, we should use the process and the team to create it. Now let us take a look at some tactics that have proven successful to actually produce one. There are entire books that you can refer to in order to go much deeper on each of these strategies, the below is meant to expose you to the flavors you will find. You may find that a few paragraphs are enough to get you started, or you may find that you want more information. Hopefully the below will point you in the right direction.

Prototyping the Vision. Much of the literature on visioning doesn't talk about vision creation; it talks about vision "discovery." That is, the vision isn't something than can be created simply through deep thought and reflection. You need to get out into the market and start looking for it; you need to discover it. The product you want to create probably doesn't already exist, and your potential customers haven't thought of it yet. In fact, if someone had thought of your product, it would likely already exist!

This is a fun situation to be in, your customers are eager to try new things, and the market is cautiously optimistic that your product will improve their lives. But you cannot go to market with vague statements and un-actionable decisions. Recently, we have seen an entire ecosystem of gadgets that help track your activity, how much you walk, sleep, run or sit still. Had these companies approached the market with the question, "Would you buy a gadget that made you healthier?" Then the answer would have been likely to be yes. But had they gone with "Would you buy something you clipped to your belt or wore around your wrist, and it counted your activity for the day?" The market would more than likely have told you no. Because of this kind of dynamic, simply asking the question isn't going to be enough. You need to show them.

This is where prototyping enters the picture. Create a version of the product that looks and feels like it should, but only has a limited feature set – or no features at all. Get to this point as quickly as possible, and release it to a group of customers. Ideally, this would be a collection of users who have opted in to being member of your "beta" community, and have signed up to take the product and provide feedback.

There is virtually no limit to what you will learn from having customers actually use the product. They will find new functions and new methods of using it, potentially even some that you hadn't conceived. For instance, people may start wearing your step-counting wristband around their ankle, or your belt clip as a pendant. Or you might find that half of them try to take a shower while still wearing it. Or any number of new experiences that would never happen without a prototype.

By creating a real, tangible product, and putting it in the market, you can begin to craft what the product should be, as well as what it should do. This method can produce a product with an optimized form and function for the market that will be using it.

Visioning through user stories. Creating your vision from prototypes allows you to continue to iterate on a product idea while finding users and market for it. Visioning by using user stories is the exact opposite; you first determine who the users are and what they are trying to do, and then you build a product around who they are and what they need.

Unlike prototyping, however, we aren't actually looking to find our users themselves, we are looking to find classes of users that might use our product. Sticking with our iPod example, we might have these kinds of users:

- An athlete who will be listening to music while training
- A mother with small children, who will be listening to sing-a-long songs in the car
- A business commuter, who will be using it on the train on the way into work
- Etc.

The goal is not to find "people" but rather to find "personas." You may even find that you give your personas names; our athlete could be Adam Athlete, our mother could be Sally Sing-a-Long, and Colleen the Commuter. Once you have this list, you can start thinking of the people behind the personas, and determine their needs, their interests, and what they might value in your product.

From here, start thinking about what the customers will do with the product, the stories that will describe the user's interactions with the product in their daily lives. Adam will frequently drop his, while Colleen needs the headphones to stay in her ears even during a bumpy train ride, etc. Sally might want to choose each song individually, while Adam wants a long playlist. Eventually, you will build up dozens of matched pairs of persona and story, and will start to have the basis of what you are going to be building. The vision of the product leads out of this exercise, and you'll find the product is much easier to "see" at this point, as you can already picture who will be using it, and what they will be doing with it.

Start with the press release. The first two strategies above start with the product and the users, respectively. You can either start with the product and find the users, or you can start with the users and build the product. A third way to craft a vision is to start from the outside looking in. What would the press release for the product look like? What would a magazine review of your product include? What type of magazine would you even want your product review in? This causes your team to stop thinking about how they view the product, and rather focus on how others would view it.

One of the important parts of this method is keeping the release brief, like a real release would be. Describe the product in 100 words or less, or even use bullet points if necessary. Choose the three to five features or attributes of the product that are worth calling out separately, and might spark someone's interest. In the end, if the release doesn't sound all that compelling to your team, it probably won't be interesting to the market, either.

This is often used as a way to back-check your vision. If you used either of the first two methods to get your vision, you probably have lots of artifacts, documents and information lying around. Your work product will also include data that you have decided not to use. It can be confusing to remember all of it. This distillation of the vision can help refocus and find where people have differences in their understanding. With so few words, you will find that you can repoint your team in the proper direction, and quickly find out if they aren't.

Focus on the remarkable. Sometimes, your product has the potential to be truly-game changing, or to be very different than anything out the market. Rather than focusing on the set of features or the kinds of customers, you may want to focus on exactly one of them. There is a company that drives a bus from Boston to New York City called the Bolt Bus. There aren't a lot of amenities, nor will you see lots of business people in suits aboard. But you can take the four-hour ride for as low as one dollar. That is pretty remarkable, but only for a very limited set of people (mostly college students), who have a narrow set of needs (be cheap.) By focusing on the one thing that makes the service different, you can build an entire business on that one thing.

This works on the high-end, as well. Tiffany sells a keychain that is no better or worse at holding keys than many other key chains. The difference is that if someone finds your keys, they can drop them in the mailbox, and Tiffany will figure out how to get them back to you. No postage needed, no addressing envelopes or phone calls. You simply register your key ring with Tiffany, and they do the rest. I suspect the use case for this very small, but the story is a great one. The care and thought that would have to occur in order for Tiffany to return your keys to you are a hint about the care and thoroughness they take in their business and their relationship with their customers.

It's much easier to be remarkable – or to produce a remarkable product – if you are willing to focus on the remarkable aspects in the first place. It's also a lot easier to get noticed when you are doing something so much better than anyone else.

Product Road Maps

Crafting the vision is an important and difficult exercise, but it's not enough to launch a successful product. Just like simply picturing yourself on a sunny beach doesn't mean you'll have a great holiday. The vision is something in the future, sometimes the distant future. You need to create a plan to get there from where you currently are. This plan is usually called a product road map.

Minimal Viable Product. Depending on the maturity of your product, you need to have different kinds of road maps. With a new product, one that hasn't hit the market yet, your sole focus should be getting the essential features and functionality out the door. Whatever is the minimal product you think that anyone in the market will buy, or even use, in order to give you direction and feedback. If a product is totally useless, you won't be able to engage customers on the level that you need to get information from them. If your product is too complete, you have invested in features before you got feedback, which is the risk that Agile seeks to avoid. Finding the line between too much and too little is an art form, and one that it critical to success. This is called the "Minimal Viable Product" or MVP.

In the pre-launch phase of your product, you should be determining what your product must do, and what it must be, in order to engage any customers. Then you create a release plan that leads up to the public release. That is, even though you aren't yet releasing to customers, you are creating complete builds that properly execute all the work done to date. Sometimes this is one release, other times it's ten. Most people suggest that you should reach MVP status around release three. That is the way to keep momentum going, and to get something into market early enough in the process to react and adjust to feedback. Some companies even number these releases using negative numbers, such as -3, -2, and -1, with release 0 being the MVP release to customers. This helps solidify the importance of the MVP release, and creates a kind of countdown that the team can follow.

On-going roadmaps. It is counterproductive to try to create a long-term road map before a product is released. At best, it will be wishful thinking, and worst, it will be describing features and functions that the market hasn't indicated that it wants. The length of your planning horizon is driven by how mature the product is, how long your lead times are between releases, and how much customer feedback is already collected. Even still, history shows that for most products, a plan that extends much past 36 months will turn out to be more fiction than helpful.

Your next few releases should be planned, the few releases after that should have thoughts already in motion, and the releases after that tend to contain "stuff to do in the future." That stuff tends to always be scheduled for the future, and will remain that way for years to come. The roadmap shouldn't be a detailed plan; it should contain the few highlights of what is coming in each release, and when it will be coming. It should be created with the team and vetted with stakeholders, but you should never feel restricted by it. Changing the plan due to customer reaction or feedback is part of the point.

I'm sure we have all seen product roadmaps that contain hundreds of lines and detailed enough to be turned directly into a project plan. That's not what a road map should be. It should describe the highlights, the release dates, and should be enough for a casual observer to understand what the future will hold. If your roadmap contains more than that, you've said too much, and limited your flexibility. Keep your stakeholders interested by giving them the highlights and the dates. That's all you need.

Anti-Patterns in Product Visions

Creating a vision seems simple. Just paint a picture of what the product could be, who will buy it, and how they'll use it. Many of them can fit on one side of a piece of paper, and contain just enough information to keep people interested. Even still, there are many places that a well-meaning product owner can go wrong. Here are a few that seem to come up frequently.

The "let's just get started" vision. I've mentioned in one of my other books, my worst professional mistake was allowing a project to begin without a clear understanding about what its goals were. The team, including the product owner, was unanimous in saying that they all knew what needed to be done, at least to reach MVP stage, and that spending effort coming up with the product vision was just a waste of time. You can probably guess it didn't go well at all. I've had product be commercial failures before, but this is the product that was biggest preventable failure of execution in my career.

There are two ways this tends to happen. In my case above, we were replacing an existing product, and the team felt that the goal of "do what it did before" was enough. Even though it is highly tempting to allow that to take the place of a good vision, it won't work in the end. The other way is what I've also called the "bottom-up" vision. That is, we didn't really have a product in mind, what we had instead was a list of features. What you wind up with is a product that is a collection of disjointed features and functionality, that don't actually aggregate into a product that makes sense. Do you really need a combination coffee maker and CD player? Of course not, but someone wanted to listen to music while waiting for their coffee to brew, so there you have it.

No matter the situation, it is never going to work out not to have an end goal in mind – or at least whatever your next goal is to be. Resist temptation to let it happen, no matter how much sense it makes. Ask your team, "If we don't know what we are doing, how will we know when we are done?"

The "let's make certain of this" vision. There is a large amount of risk involved in launching a new product to the market. Agile attempts to mitigate this risk by launching early, engaging customers, getting their feedback, and reacting. Another way that companies attempt to mitigate this risk is through extensive research and analysis.

Clearly, doing some market research, understanding the customers, and doing diligent analysis are important in business. If you do not perform any analysis, then you have very little hope of creating an MVP that is accepted by the market at all. It is critical to pay attention not only to what and how much research and analysis you are doing, it's also vital to understand why you are doing it.

By nature, many companies are risk-adverse. They believe that if you spend enough time at the beginning of a project, then you have a high likelihood of producing the perfect product the first time and never having a need to go back and change direction. Your finance department will be asking for up to three years of forecasts for sales and profits generated, and guidance is sometimes given to executives or stockholders based on products that don't yet exist. Agile believes this is a riskier path than failing the first time.

The chances of being totally right with the first iteration is virtually nil. The odds of getting to a good product that customers love, and makes a healthy margin for the company are much better if the team is allow to test, learn, adapt and change along the way. By spending too much time doing research and analysis, you are stealing time away from the team to do the real learning.

Performing solid analysis is key and must be done. But you should always be seeking to launch as soon as you have an MVP. The only real way to learn what the market is going to want is to give them something to react to. And you do that by showing them what you've got.

The "faster horses" vision. There is a quote attributed to Henry Ford that states, "If I had asked people what they wanted, they would have said faster horses." It seems to be unlikely that Mr. Ford actually uttered those words, but the idea still sticks in the minds of innovators everywhere. While it does indeed take a delicate balance of arrogance and brilliance to bring a disruptive product to market, if that's all you have to rely upon, then your chances of success go down considerably.

Some companies believe that they know what their customers want and need much more than even their customers do. The few times that this strategy worked is unfortunately celebrated in the media, and is often only visible in hindsight. Once an unexpected success is wildly popular, it's a lot easier to say that the team didn't need to consult with the market. Trying to innovate without any input is more likely to end up in failure.

The way to prevent this is fairly obvious. Include your customers and users into the process. Let them see early releases, provide feedback, and play with releases. The team is always empowered to completely ignore comments from customers, but they shouldn't be empowered to never seek it in the first place.

The "everything for everyone" vision. Elsewhere in this chapter, we discuss the concept of user stories and personas. When creating your MVP, product owners often choose to launch with a minimal set of functionality for a single persona. Other times, product owners elect to go public when they have the minimal features needed for several of their personas. This allows the target customer base to start engaging and provide feedback on the product.

Some companies seem unwilling to trust the process; that to launch with limited functionality or for only a few segments of the customer base isn't acceptable. They feel like feedback gathered on an incomplete product isn't valid, and that without a fully-formed product in the market, there is no way to know how well you are doing. This kind of attitude is acceptable in Agile, as any release is better than no release, but it will have a very high probability of causing waste and changing the return on investment for your development team.

This anti-pattern could also be called an MVP, or a "Maximally Viable Product." That is, it's the full set of features that the product owner believes is needed to be a complete solution for customer needs. Doing this will delay your initial launch, robbing your team of valuable time to make improvements to the product. It will also waste resources, as you continue to develop without getting feedback. Attempting to be everything to everyone, at initial launch, will leave you with an underwhelming product in the end.

Chapter 3

Creating the Product Backlog

Traditional project and product management creates a veritable mountain of documents. There are requirements documents, specification documents, brand documents, feature documents, etc. Writing these documents is a difficult and lengthy task, and it is a task that never ends, as the documents continually need updating throughout the project. The first time someone reads something that contains outdated or incorrect information they will stop considering it a valid source of product information

Agile is sometimes incorrectly assumed to be to the exact opposite extreme – no documentation. Much like the "let's just get started" anti-pattern, this is not the case. If the product owner cannot even express what it is they want build, the nothing will ever get built. Instead, most Agile methodologies use a single artifact, and use it to specify everything about the project. It is known as the "Product Backlog."

The concept of the backlog is fairly easy to grasp; it is a listing of all outstanding work for the product, listed in priority order. Note the word "work" in that sentence; and work can take many forms. It can contain development tasks, customer research and interviews, buying a coffee maker, setting up the team room, or creating your build environment. This is the primary, and sometimes only, document in an Agile project. It is therefore critical to understand how to properly use and care for it.

Attributes of a Product Backlog

In traditional project management documents tended to have a single purpose and everything was viewed through that perspective. This means that the requirements specification document was primarily focused on the requirements, and could safely ignore speaking to other parts of the product. There would then be a different document that would cover those other topics. This meant to get a full picture of what needed to be done you may have to read several documents, each of them showing you a different viewpoint.

Agile thinks this is wasteful. The product backlog is meant to hold items that contain all the information you will need about a requirement or user story. It can therefore be examined all at once, and everything that is important to know about it can be seen together. The four things that a good backlog must be are properly detailed, sized, prioritized, and flexible.

The properly detailed backlog. Another difference between traditional requirements and Agile requirements is the strategy on how detailed requirements need to be. A traditional requirements document would go into as much detail as the product owner can think of at the time of writing. In some cases, this will be to an incredibly fine level of specification. In others, the product owner will merely put a "TBD" in the spot, and leave it for later. Even the highest level of detail is often not enough to actually deliver something, and rarely does someone go back and clean up the document and go back and clean all those TBDs.

The product backlog is a stack of items, with those with the highest priority at the top, and those with the lowest priority at the bottom. Attempting to detail each of them out to a medium-high level would be wasteful, and often whatever you would write would be wrong anyway. Items at the bottom of the stack might never get done, so time spent on detailing them out is not a good use of effort. Items at the top are ready to be worked on right now, so if they are not complete the team will sit idle while you finish up your work.

Proper backlog detailing means not attempting to tackle the entire stack and getting everything minimally specified. It means spending no time at all on the items on the bottom of the list, and to reinvest that time in the things on the top of the list. This way, the right amount of effort is being spent on the right things.

Sizing items. The concept of spending more time on high-priority items than low-priority items seems obvious. But there is another dimension that you must consider, and that is the effort or cost associated with an item. If something is very low cost, then its priority might be very high. Conversely, if it is high cost, they you might never get that feature into the product at all. Without knowing the size of the backlog items, it is very difficult to decide where they should be on the list.

Size can mean several things. It can mean development effort, or it can mean actual dollars spent to do something. It can also mean elapsed time or several other metrics that equate to project cost. Agile has a simple, and rather powerful way of detailing these out which we will discuss a bit later. But note that doing proper sizing is very similar to doing proper detailing. The highest needs should have the highest confidence cost estimate.

Items in your backlog that are not sized are essentially placeholders. Having these is fine, but they should be placed at the bottom of the list. Items without a size cannot be actioned, and therefore will fall below even the lowest properly sized item. If the product owner wants something done, getting it sized is critical to having it fall in its proper place in the backlog.

Prioritized. The first three of these qualities all work together. In order to understand an item, it needs to be detailed out to the proper level, then it needs to be sized, and then its priority needs to be reset. As the project moves forward and more about the product is learned and discovered, there will be constant cycles of detailing, scoping and prioritizing. But without prioritization the whole scheme falls apart.

Initially, prioritization gets set based on how important the product owner believes the item to be. This can even be a guess; in Agile, the product owner has final say on priority. It shouldn't be done in complete isolation, however. Certain things on the backlog will be out of your area of expertise, or perhaps you won't have the right perspective to know just how important something is to the end product.

Be prepared to perform an initial prioritization on everything in the backlog, using literal numbers. And note that there can be no tie scores. While certainly there are things that all must be done before the product can ship, that doesn't mean they are all the #1 priority. The team must know what to work on first, second and third. You might know that the product cannot be launched until numbers one through seventeen are complete, but the team needs to know what to do right now. Prioritization is the mechanism that drives this.

Flexible. This is a statement just as much about the product owner as about the backlog items. As a best practice, the product owner is the one and only person who can prioritize items in the backlog. They get final say on what to work on next, and what will languish at the bottom of the list. But that does not give license to the product owner to be stubborn and refuse input from others.

As the project moves forward, you and the team will be constantly learning and discovering new things. New items will be added to the backlog, and other items will be taken away. Customers, executives and users will provide feedback. All of this will require the backlog (and its owner) to be flexible and responsive to new input.

There are things that many people don't like in traditional project management. Agile seeks to replace them with things that we do like, and that we think work better. Ignoring them, or wishing that they will go away, is not a winning strategy. Remain flexible, remain responsive, and you will be living in the principles that Agile hopes you will follow.

Working with the Product Backlog

The product backlog is the single most important artifact in the entire project, and the product owner alone owns it. Unlike traditional management, where there can be dozens of documents that are all left to atrophy and become irrelevant, in Agile, the product backlog needs constant attention, affection, and maintenance. This act of keeping the backlog current and relevant is known as "Backlog Grooming."

There are four primary tasks that go into grooming the backlog. They are:

- Adding new items and removing old ones
- Ensuring full detailing of high priority items
- Ensuring proper sizing and estimation on items
- Prioritizing and reprioritizing the items

The product owner is the primary person responsible for all of the above tasks, but there is no way that product owner can do it alone. Grooming the backlog is a task that has to be done with the entire team, in fact some high-performing teams estimate that as much as 20% of the time is spent on backlog grooming. The backlog is thus written and maintained by everyone on the team, and not just the product owner. This is a vital difference from the days when the business owner would write requirements and hand them off to be delivered.

Throughout this book, we have discussed the importance of removing barriers between the business of the product and the development of the product. In all cases, creating of an "Us vs. Them" scenario will lead to a bad result. Grooming the backlog is a very good way to break this barrier. Involving the team in what is being worked on, and what those things mean, bring the development team into the business, and the business team into the development. It creates a mutual sense of ownership that will go a long way to success in the end.

There are many ways to set your grooming calendar. Some teams like to do it daily, for an hour or less, just to keep on top of things and make it a daily routine. Other teams like to dedicate a half day or more to it during each cycle. In the end, it really doesn't matter, as long as you establish a cadence, and keep to it. Having buy-in on the backlog is the goal; what process your team chooses to get there is not all that important.

Adding and organizing items

As the project progresses, you and the team will learn more about the product, the market and the marketplace than you knew before you began. Because of this, in the initial phases of the project, you will find yourself adding more items to the backlog than you are removing. If you come from an environment where you were expected to know everything about the product ahead of time, then you are probably in for a surprise. Product requirements are never frozen, they are merely deemed good enough to proceed.

As the understanding of the product, the customers and the market improves, so does the product backlog. This means that requirements much change, new ones will be created, and old ones retired. This will happen throughout the entire lifecycle of the project, not just at the beginning stages. Most managers accustomed to traditional methods will have a desire to write down everything they know, and take guesses at the rest. Agile tells you not to do this, but to keep learning and refining as you go. The change in mindset is difficult, but powerful once you get the hang of it.

Entering new items. In traditional product management, the product manager is required to think up everything they thing they want their product to be, all at once. Changes later are difficult, expensive, and discouraged. Agile has the opposite viewpoint; changes are expected, easy, and encouraged. But you cannot proceed with an empty backlog; you must seed the list with things you have a reasonable level of confidence in. Without an initial list, there is nothing to change later.

At the beginning of the project, the product owner should be focused on the requirements necessary to create the Minimal Viable Product. Starting without at least the minimum amount of requirements will lead to significant doubt in the product, just as starting with too much will create an unwieldy and confusing list. Focus only on the critical needs, and leave all the other requirements, no matter how clever or interesting, aside for now.

The items in the backlog should be detailed out commensurate with their priority. High priority items should be analyzed enough to get the key points highlighted, while low priority items should be left as high level requirements for later. Creating this initial list will allow the team to properly groom the backlog, where new items will be created, unnecessary items will be removed, and existing items will be further detailed to make them real.

Once the backlog is seeded, it is important not to place too much weight on the items that were entered in this initial phase. Just because a requirement was entered at the beginning only meant that it was viewed as necessary at the time – given further reflection, this may not turn out to be the case. Consider the entire backlog whenever you are adding new items; if a new idea seems more important than something that has been on the list for months, that is okay. The more important item should always be prioritized higher, no matter if it was thought up yesterday or last year.

As the team gets more comfortable with the product and the customer needs, the requirements will become more relevant. It is quite possible that the newer requirements are actually more on target than the initial ones, due to new knowledge or a better understanding of the product. It is the product owner's job to understand this critical difference.

Detailing out items. Agile is specifically vague about how backlog items should be detailed. Many teams find that using the concepts of "epics" and "user stories" gets them to the right level of detail, depending on the situation and the priority.

Epics are very high-level descriptions of a whole class of activities that the product should allow the user to perform. Usually, they are so broad that they aren't actionable on their own. "Allow a customer to buy something" can be an epic, but there is no way to write that in such a way that a developer could develop it, or someone could decide if it were properly created.

User Stories are much more descriptive, and try to describe what a user would be doing in order to achieve a part of the overall epic. A single epic can spawn multiple user stories, but each story should be complete and have an easy to understand success criteria. The higher up the priority list an epic gets, the more likely it is that it should be broken up into stories that can be developed and understood.

Epics and user stories are not the only artifacts that an agile team can produce. There can be descriptions of users, story boards and story descriptions, business rules that are invisible to the user, UX interactions and other prototypes. These artifacts are not intended to be used instead of the backlog, but rather to enhance it and help clarify what the backlog items mean. Usually a team will only invest time in clarifying items that either need clarity, or are high on the prioritization list. This helps to prevent wasting effort on items that either don't need attention, or aren't worthy of the extra effort.

Using Themes. We have discussed two sizes of items above, the epic and the user story. Several user stories make up an epic, and they can all be described, developed and implemented independently. Similarly, several epics can make up a Theme, and each epic can be developed and deployed on its own. In usual practice, themes are the least detailed unit of description, and are used to hold other items in the backlog.

Imagine you are creating a new gaming console. One of the themes you would like to develop is the ability to play online with or against your friends. This theme of playing online can itself be broken up into several epics, which can then be broken up into several user stories. However, you may decide that your console can be launched into the market without any of this functionality at all. This is how themes can be a powerful backlog management tool.

Themes allow the project team to talk about whole sections of functionality without having to talk about specific stories. Using our "play online" example, that may have four epics, and 20 user stories that compose the full theme. This allows the team to talk about all 20 stories at once, and if the decision is made that this functionality isn't critical for launch, than all the work associated with that theme can be easily reprioritized.

This turns out to also be a very good way for humans to organize their thoughts about the product, as well. Stories tend to be difficult to describe in shorthand, epics are slightly easier, and themes are meant to be short enough to understand with just a few words. You may find that some of your stories don't naturally map to a theme, and this is okay. However, resist the urge to have a theme named something like "other." Better to leave your stories or epics orphaned, than to have themes that don't make any logical sense.

Prioritizing Items

One of my favorite Dilbert cartoons shows Dilbert at a white board with three words on it: Essential, Critical and Must-Have. Dilbert then cheekily asks, "Let me know which group I should stop working on." I break this cartoon out at the beginning of most projects. One of my old bosses even used to council product teams "if it makes things easier, use the auto-numbering function in your email client." I never went quite that far; people know how to make a list. What they don't know how to do is to properly prioritize items.

They key thing to know about prioritization is that it's relative, not absolute. Certainly, an automobile needs an engine, steering wheel and brakes in order to be useful at all. But if you don't have a method of propulsion, you probably have little need for a way to steer it or stop it. All those things are vital to proper operation of the car, but they aren't equally important.

Prioritization does not drive the decision about what is in the product and what is out, it is guidance to the team on what to work on first, and then what to work on after that is complete. If the backlog isn't appropriately prioritized, or if all items are given the same priority, then your team will work on things in whatever order makes the most sense to them. In many cases, this will work out just fine. But it is your job as product owner to make sure the team doesn't need to guess.

Prioritization is often best done with the entire team present. Not only does this use the collective intelligence of the team, but it also creates a sense of understanding not only for the priorities, but also the rationale behind them. You will find that your team works better when they understand and had a hand in deciding what they would be working on.

Setting priorities not only decides what will get developed first, it also decides how much attention something gets. High priority items on the backlog should get more attention during grooming meetings, and they should be getting more and more detailed and specific as they near the top of the list. Conversely, low priority items won't get much attention at all, which is exactly what you want. This will prevent the team from spending much effort on something that might never be needed, or needs more input from customer or from outside research.

When setting priorities, it's often easiest to start at the top and work down. This means prioritizing the themes, then the epics, and then the stories. It's a lot easier to put the themes in priority order than it is to put the user stories in order. A high priority theme for our game console might be "plays games." That certainly feels more important than "streams video from the web." Compare this to the user stories of "supports wireless controllers" and "supports all major formats of streaming video." A case could be made that the latter is more important than the former, but not if the priorities of the themes are properly set. The highest priority story on a low priority theme should be viewed with skepticism before any work begins on it.

Prioritizing by business value. One of the more basic ways to prioritize items is by value. It's somewhat obvious to say that the team should be working on the most valuable items first. However, determining value turns out to be a tricky problem.

If your product is in the pre-launch stage, then the priority has to be set based on how important the item is for launch, and no other metric. I worked for an e-commerce company that launched several new products and product categories in a very short time. Each product launch had a task named something like "include the product in the site taxonomy." This was a mundane, not very difficult task. And there is no way that anyone would view it has a high-value item.

However, without doing it, there would be no way for customers to find the product; it would gate the launch of the product if it was not completed as we would not be able to sell any of the new products. This meant that this relatively easy task was very high on the priority list. And that was the right decision, indeed.

As you are examining items for prioritization, think if the user could still achieve their goals without this functionality. This will help the team focus on developing only the features that are truly needed for each release. If a different method of achieving the goal exists, or if there is an alternative that gets them close, it might be worth delaying this item till a future release. Even releasing a product with annoying, but functional, functionality can be better than waiting until you have the perfect solution. The goal is to ship your product, get feedback, and adjust. You can't do that if you wait till you have everything ready from the start.

This level of rigor should be applied to old requirements as well as new ones. Just because a requirement was added a long time ago, and deemed vital for launch at the time doesn't mean that it is still the case. After some of the product has been built and the team gains a level of comfort with what the customers are going to need, new solutions will emerge that may be better than what was originally proposed. It is often the case that old requirements are not as well-formed or as well understood as new ones, and the newer ones can obviate the need for the old ones. Agile is a process of constant re-examination and re-prioritization; nothing should get "grandfathered" in.

I'm tempted to make the clever rhyme, "When in doubt, leave it out." Luckily, this is exactly the right sentiment. If you are unsure if a piece of functionality is truly vital, then you should consider leaving it out of the release entirely. The point of Agile is to ship the product early and often, and learn from feedback from the market. If you aren't sure if something is important, ship without it, and see if the customers complain. If they don't, then you didn't waste any effort producing functionality that wouldn't drive value. If they do, then you will be developing it with the conviction that you know the customers are asking for it. Either way, you get the right answer, and do the right thing.

Prioritizing by risk. Projects are full of risky items. When we talk about risk, there are two main flavors: implementation risk, and commercial risk. The former asks the question "Can this be done at all?" These are the types of risks that software engineers are quite accustomed to mitigating. They build prototypes, tests, mockups and the like, all as a proof-of-concept that the product itself is possible. Even though Agile does support the idea of prioritizing based on implementation risk, this isn't the kind of risk that Agile was meant to address.

Agile was primarily constructed to help with commercial risk. In many ways, this is more accurately termed uncertainty risk or requirements risk. The product owner has some idea that the product will work in the market, but isn't certain. Details such as pricing, service, features included, user experience and lots of other things cannot be known ahead of time, and will never be known without allowing the customers to weigh in. The sooner the product is able to get into user's hands, the sooner the product team can get feedback on the product and the offering, and determine if adjustments needs to be made. Due to this, teams will often prioritize risky items highly, and develop and release them first.

This is a duel-edged sword for most teams. On one hand, by releasing their risk items first, the team can get feedback early, change course if needed, and prove or disprove their hypotheses quickly. If the initial thinking turns out to be wrong, then not a lot of effort or budget was expended on tasks that might not drive meaningful value. On the other hand, by releasing risk items first, the project is likely to begin with a string of failures. A high-performing Agile team embraces this notion; the concept of "failing fast" is a key tenet of the movement. Better to know you are on the wrong track as soon as possible, rather than expending effort building a product that no one wants. But not all organizations are wired this way.

If the product starts with a string of successes by launching the least risky things first, then the failures can still be waiting deeper in the project. Some organizations will reward this; the project will be deemed as to have been doing so well, but then a few unforeseen events came up that turned the project into a failure. This is a tough organization to be agile within, as the argument can be made that this failure could have been avoided. If you are truly going to follow the process, and make an attempt to launch a product that people will love, saving the things you are uncertain about is the wrong thing to do.

Prioritize by speed to market. In the same general concept as prioritizing by uncertainty risk, some teams will prioritize the backlog entirely based on what can be released first. If something can be built and released in a few weeks, teams will prioritize it over a more valuable feature that will take months to put together. There is some merit in this approach, as the sooner you get something into the market, the sooner you will begin learning which path your product should take next.

One of the problems with doing this is that you wind up with data that is not totally reliable. If a feature from the middle of the priority list is released early, customers can be disappointed that the critical functionality isn't available. You will then find out that your customers are disappointed in the product, even though they may be happy with the feature itself. This may generate comments, but not ones that are actionable to the product team.

Speed to market tends to be a good tie-breaker. If two items have a similar perceived value, or if you aren't certain about which should be developed first, then choosing the one that can be completed first is a valid approach. Using it as a primary driver of prioritization can lead to wasted time, as well as putting the wrong product in the market.

Prioritizing by project sequence. One of the tasks of a project manager is to identify dependencies between project tasks, and sequencing their delivery in such a way that pre-requisites are done in time for features to be developed. There are entire artifacts and strategies around mapping the project sequence appropriately. There are Gantt charts, critical paths, and entire project plans that are meant to track tasks, dependencies and other parts of the plan. If you are accustomed to this, you may prioritize your backlog this way; you may prioritize the pre-requisites for other items highly, so that they are ready when the time comes. This isn't the right thing to do.

Having dependencies are the exact opposite mindset that Agile attempts to impart. They reduce flexibility, they create barriers to working, and they wind up creating uncertainty when creating estimates. A user story might be worth 5 points if done after another, but 13 points if done before. Therefore, the same piece of functionality can have very different estimates, which makes it impossible to properly prioritize. Because of this, breaking or resolving dependencies are important to being able to act in an agile fashion.

Take for example paying for an item on an ecommerce site. We have two user stories, pay with credit card, or pay with PayPal. Built into these stories is a generic "process customer payment" story that should apply to both. The two acceptable ways to remove dependencies are either to combine them all, or split them all apart.

By combining all these items, you wind up with a story that sounds like "pay for an item." And in it, you have paying via PayPal, credit card, ACH and any other payment method you want, as well as the ability to process the payment. While this does successfully break the dependency, it creates a task that is probably too big to work on and too unwieldy to prioritize. The other way to handle this is to break everything smaller. This still causes a bit of a problem; pay by credit card still relies upon the "process payment" story. However, each payment method story is now completely independent from each other, and each has their own estimate that won't change depending on the order they are done in. This allows the product owner to launch with just credit card, and delay the other options for a later release. If it's all done as one story, there is way to do this.

Planning Cycles

Depending on the actual flavor of Agile that your team is using, you may call the planning cycle by a different name. Sometimes they will be called sprints, other times they will be called iterations. Some organizations will just call them versions, and number them from one to infinity. Vocabulary does matter a bit in this business, but not enough that anyone should enforce any name on the concept of determining what to do, doing it, and then looking back on what you have done. No matter what form of Agile you are using, you must have all three things.

The only word that you want to stay away from with this concept is the word "release." In most Agile literature and teams, a release is something that is actually released to the public. Several iterations, sprints or whatever your teams calls them are what make up a release. For our purposes, I'm simply going to call them cycles.

And the first thing you need to do when planning for a cycle, is to determine the goal you are trying to achieve.

Defining the goal of the cycle. As you have probably figured out by now, one of the tenets of Agile development is to understand your goal before you start doing anything. If you do not know what you are doing, then there is no way to know if you are doing it right.

The goal of a development cycle should be to move the product closer to being able to be released to customers. A good goal is both achievable and meaningful; it must be a goal that isn't vague like "improve the customer experience," but it should be substantial enough to guide the team's actions during the cycle. The goal should be reachable, even if all the items in the backlog are not completed. If removing a single story from the cycle completely invalidates the goal, then your goal isn't broad enough.

The cycle goal cannot be done by the product owner in complete isolation. Like all other tasks, the more that the entire team is involved, the better the outcome will be, and the more committed the team will be to achieving that outcome. It also helps focus the team on the items in the backlog that help reach the goal. If there are items that people are working on that won't help with reaching the goal, they should stop working on them. It's the goal that helps facilitate this discussion.

Identifying and communicating the goal can and should require changes the product backlog. Items on the top of the backlog that don't help reach the goal should be demoted, just as items that are lower on the priority list that are critical for the goal should be lifted. Once the goal has been identified and agreed upon, the backlog should be adjusted to match. You should never have conflicts in priority between what you are trying to achieve in a cycle and the priorities on the backlog. Doing so will just cause confusion in the team.

Preparing for the Cycle. Once you choose the goal for the cycle, you need to focus on specifying all the items that help reach the goal, even at the expense of other items. This means you need to identify the items that will be in the cycle and doing all you can to get them ready to be developed, while ignoring those that are not in the cycle, no matter their overall priority. This takes discipline from the product owner; often something in a future cycle is critical for the product, but needs to be ignored for now. It can be difficult to reconcile this in your head, but it is indeed the right thing to do.

Usually, you are choosing epics, or parts of epics, to include in a cycle. In order to make these items actionable, you need to make sure they are properly broken down into units that can be fully developed, tested and deployed. Properly decomposing an epic can take several iterations; for a specific cycle, the goal is to make sure that everything on the list is ready to be developed.

The amount of items in any specific iteration is wildly variable, and depends on the team. Teams develop something called "velocity," which is a measure of how much the team can accomplish in a single cycle. Lots of things go into this calculation, including team size, skills and expertise, the quality of the technology, as well as their confidence in the requirements. As a product owner, you should understand what the velocity of your team is, and prepare enough work for them to develop, and perhaps a little bit more. If the team generally delivers 20 story points worth of work each cycle, you probably want to prepare 25 or 30 points worth of work. This will give the team flexibility to move items around, and will allow you to take advantage of situations where items turned out to be easier than originally thought.

In an Agile development project, there is little attention paid to how much work remains. Since you are actively developing the product, new requirements are being generated, new things are being learned, and new ideas are coming to life. Trying to measure how much there is left to do is a fool's errand – the more that you accomplish, there more there is remaining to do. It will seem that at early stages of the product, you are further behind than when you started!

Teams will and should measure themselves based on what has been accomplished. Agile values items that have been developed and shipped to customers considerably higher than items that are partially developed, even if those are larger. Therefore, it is your responsibility as product owner to break items down into units than can be developed and completed within the span of a cycle.

Decomposing user stories. We have already talked about the three major units when it comes to gathering requirements: themes, epics and stories. In order for requirements to be made real for developers, they need to be broken down until they are able to developed in a single cycle. The actual work required to decompose requirements into developable units may take more than one cycle. This is expected and okay; the goal is to have user stories ready to be developed in time for the team to begin. If this takes weeks or months, that's perfectly normal.

Agile has two main enemies when it comes to user stories: non-specificity and size. Stories that are vague or leave a lot of details out are useless to a developer. At best, the developer will simply skip over your story, and work on something else. At worst, the developer will try to guess what it is that you wanted and try to fill in the missing details themselves. Consider our ecommerce example above; we have a user story called "pay for item." This might make sense to the product owner, and it even makes logical sense when you are reading it. But once you sit down to actually do the work, you find that there is so much involved with the story that there is no way to understand it all without further breaking it down.

That brings us to the size of a story. Recall that we are specifying work to be done in a single cycle. Best practice in Agile is to have cycles last no longer than a month; many teams prefer cycles that are much shorter, perhaps as short as a week. If an item is too big to be developed in a single cycle, then you are creating even more work for your team. Not only must they develop the feature, but they also must figure out how to carry it from one cycle to the next.

One way to view this is to consider the acceptance criteria for the story. Many teams will call this the "definition of done." It is a list of things that the feature must do in order to be considered complete. As this list gets long (more than a dozen items) or if the list starts to include new requirements, such as the need to pay with a gift card, then your story is almost certainly too big, and should be decomposed further.

Estimating Story Sizes

There is a small chicken-and-egg problem when it comes to prioritizing a backlog. You need to know how much effort something will take before you can choose a priority, yet we have already described not wasting time estimating items that aren't at the top of the backlog. It can be a conundrum.

Many Agile methodologies have a lightweight solution for estimating that can be used in a two-pass fashion. In order to do any prioritization at all, you need to create rough estimates out of the themes, epics and stories. Once you have things roughly sized, you should expect to go back over them and turn the rough estimates into more detailed ones. In the process of doing so, you will continue to decompose the stories and change their priorities. The more you groom your backlog, the better everyone will understand it, the higher the quality of the items will become.

There are many ways to estimate the size of items, but I'm only going to cover the one that is an Agile innovation, Story Points.

Using Story Points. Story points are very simple, yet very powerful, nuanced and complex. They rely upon the theory that says that your first instinct when it comes to a decision is probably the right one. In Malcom Gladwell's book, <u>Blink</u>, he discusses the notion of thinking without thinking. It is exactly this power than story points attempt to harness, and they work wonderfully. They are also very intuitive to use; you can usually make a decision instantly, and be correct a large majority of the time.

There are two key features of story points. First, they use an arbitrary value which doesn't necessarily map back to something real, like hours or days spent. Second, they are a relative value, not an absolute one. This means that each team can have a different scale to use, and the method still holds. We mentioned the concept of velocity before – how many story points a team believes they can accomplish in a single cycle. One team can have a velocity of 20, while another has velocity of 50, even though they are accomplishing the *same* amount of work. This is what makes them so simple, they are quick responses that are customized to your team.

Teams also find that they have used these before without knowing it. For instance, teams will have used "t-shirt sizes" in the past, labelling features as XS, S, M, L or XL. Even without attempting to define what "M" means, most developers are able to distinguish an S from an XL, or even an XS from an S.

A fairly common practice is to use a modified Fibonacci sequence, and add some values at the high end. Stories aren't quite given "t-shirt sizes" they are instead given a number that represents the number of points a story is worth, in effort. Usually a team uses one of the follow values: {1, 2, 3, 5, 8, 13, 20, 40, 100.} The values of 40 and 100 are not really useful for estimation, as they really mean "too big" or "way too big." Even the value of 20 is generally considered to be too high for most teams to execute on.

The key thing to understand is that these are not meant to represent anything like effort-days, line of code, function points, or any other metric to which you may be accustomed. They are meant to be a relative measure of how much work can be accomplished in a single cycle. This estimate is meant to be all-in, and include development, testing, analysis or any other task that it will take to get the work done. As long as a story rated 5 points is roughly the same as any other story with the same value, and is more than the ones lower, and less than the ones higher, then your estimates are being done properly. It doesn't matter if the items are diverse; you can easily have a 5-point story of pure development, as well as another one that is purely analysis, or even setting up the build environment. However the team decides to use story points, they will be fine as long as they remain consistent.

Playing Planning Poker. Story points are relative to each other, and specific to the team. So then how can a new team or someone new to a team, ever properly estimate something? Agile works best when the entire team is involved in everything; the methodology believes that the person doing the work should have been involved in doing the estimating and even in discovering the requirements. Therefore, we needed a lightweight way for everyone on the team to be involved in estimating every backlog item without causing a massive undertaking and amount of work. Planning Poker[6] was created to fulfill this need.

While no actual gambling is involved, there is a sense of fun and excitement in the process. While doing cycle planning, each team member is given a deck of cards with the Fibonacci numbers mentioned above printed on them. Most decks include 10 cards for the values between 1 and 100, some include only eight, some may have other values. The idea is that each team member has a full set of each valid story point value in their hand in front of them. From here, estimating the work is done collaboratively with the entire team.

The product owner is responsible for describing the story, deciding on what the acceptance criteria would be, and answering any questions. Clarifying conversations are fine to have, but solution design is not done at this point. Recall, the

---

[6] http://www.planningpoker.com/

goal is to be able to get through as much of the backlog as possible; digging deeply into each story will prevent that.

At this point, each team member makes a hidden decision for how many points the story will be worth by placing the appropriate card face down. This is done without any assumptions, including knowledge of which developer or developers would do the work. Once each member has made their decision, all cards are flipped up. If all the estimates are the same or reasonably close, then a consensus can often be reached, and the team can move on to the next item. If one or more of the estimates differ wildly, then the people who have the outlying opinions should talk for a few minutes about why they disagree with the team. After this time, the team votes again. The cycles continue until a consensus is reached or the estimates all come out the same.

Three things must be true for the team to be able to estimate an item. The team must have an understanding for what needs to be delivered, any dependencies or roadblocks need to be uncovered, and the acceptance criteria must be understandable and specific. This includes the criteria that the story does not need to meet, in order to be declared done. If any of these three things fail, then either new backlog items need to be created to get the information, or the item needs to be further broken down so that it is easier to understand and estimate.

To help ensure accuracy, the estimates should be back-tested. Once more than a couple of items have been sized, then new ones should be tested against older ones, to see if everyone still agrees with the values. Once you have a stable of stories of a certain size, you may find that one or more need to be increased or decreased. Not only will this give the team more accurate estimates, but it will also give the team a level of comfort with the plan.

It is also important to note that the best practice in Agile is to only allow people involved with the development of the story to estimate it. This includes developers, testers, analysts, or anyone who will actually be producing the story. This means that the product owner, project manager, ScrumMaster, or anyone not involved in the actual creation of the item does not get a vote. Everyone should be at the discussion and participate, but only those who are doing the work are allowed to set the estimates.

Handling very large backlogs

In a previous chapter, we discussed how to handle very large projects by using separate teams and creating the role of a Chief Product Owner. This works great when there are separate work streams, or the teams can be divided in a logical way. But this is not always the case; sometimes what you really have is one team with a very large backlog that needs to be managed. To help manage this complexity, many teams spend more time in grooming and provide specific views into the backlog for easier management.

Changing grooming timelines. Normal practice has the team grooming the backlog items that are likely to be in the next cycle, and perhaps a few more. If the backlog is sufficiently large, this will leave you with a long list of items that are vague and misunderstood. If you are in this situation, the team should still focus on grooming the items likely to make the next development cycle. But more time should be spent on items further down in the list, so that more items can be detailed and understood.

Doing this means that you increase the percentage of the backlog that has been specified, which will give the team a level of comfort with the items to come. It also provides for a bigger list of ready-to-go stories, so that if there either an opportunity to pull in new work, or if the priority of the business changes, there are enough items ready for the team to work on. By expanding the number of cycles you are working on specifying, you will wind up with a better groomed and more manageable backlog, no matter the size.

Using Theme-specific backlogs. It is important for an Agile team to have one and only one backlog. This allows for visibility and ensuring that product prioritization is done on the product as the whole, and not just for local needs. It can be helpful, however, to provide views or filters on the backlog that allow you to look at it on the theme level, rather on than on the product level.

It's possible and quite valid for a theme to be broken up into several stories, each of which are then prioritized in the backlog. If the backlog has a huge amount of items, however, you wind up with difficulty if you want to shift things around based on themes. For instance, if the highest priority story for a certain theme becomes impossible, the product owner might want to elevate the priority of the next highest story for that theme. Without a representation of the backlog by theme, this is very difficult to do, and even more difficult to understand.

This kind of scheme can also work with multiple product owners, but it's not required to be done that way. A single product owner can work with the backlogs separately, prioritizing them, grooming them, and determining the acceptance criteria based on the themes. Keeping the top stories ready to go in each theme means there is always work to do in all areas. Conversely, actively deciding not to groom items in a theme calls into question the overall priority of the theme itself. Finally, it is possible for all the stories in a theme to be prioritized low on the list. Without being able to look at the backlog by theme, items and entire themes can be lost.

Anti-Patterns in Backlog Management

The backlog is a simple tool. It is really just a prioritized listing of items that the product owner wants developed. It turns out that it can be very difficult to use properly. The tool is deceptive, in that product owners often want to compliment the backlog with other items, or make it much bigger than necessary, or doesn't keep the backlog healthy. Constant attention paid to backlog hygiene will do more for the success of a project than having all the right ideas from the start.

Using the backlog as documentation. I've seen new product owners try to create a backlog by first creating a requirements document, and then translating that into backlog items. This actually seems like it should work; most requirements documents are neatly numbered and spell out exactly what needs to be done. Some of them will even go four or five levels deep in requirements (1.2.5.2.1(c), for instance) which looks like it maps directly to a backlog item.

Not only does it not work, it actually belies a dangerous misunderstanding.

Backlog items should be atomic. Meaning, stories should be continually broken down until they can be prioritized individually, developed on their own, and provide meaningful value even if they are the only things that make it into a certain release. By taking a large requirements document and merely breaking it into pieces you won't get this. What you will get instead is a set of inter-dependent requirements that either aren't complete on their own, or they necessitate a specific ordering of execution. This is the opposite of Agile.

Seeing a backlog that looks like this tends to be a sign of a product owner that doesn't believe in many of the Agile tenets. In particular, the notion of discovering and refining requirements while the project is in motion. If the product owner believes they are able to know all that there is to know before the project begins, enough to write an entire specification document, then it may be a sign that the product owner is unwilling to be flexible when it comes to modifying them. Even if the product owner is ready to make changes as time passes, there will be a level of friction based on the fact that many of the items are already fully specified. This is not a good sign for the team.

Finally, requirements specifications are often used to counter a lack of a product vision. If a product owner does not have a good idea for the overall concept of the product, they generally do have thoughts about the specifics they want. Sometimes, they will go ahead and start crafting the requirements that they do know about, and hope that an overall vision will appear out of the details. This sometimes works, but even when it does, it's mostly by accident.

If you see a backlog that looks a lot like a requirements specification broken into pieces, there are a lot of things that could be wrong. As a product owner, you are signaling to your team that all the requirements are known, so working in an agile fashion is not necessary. In reality, you could be way off, severely limiting your chances of success.

The Shopping List backlog. As projects get created and funded, they can sometimes change direction and shape dramatically. One thing that can happen is a series of loosely connected requirements can be put together to create project that hopes to gain economies of scale. At a previous company, the product owners decided to combine creating luggage tags with Christmas ornaments, using the logic that they are both "things that get hung on other things." This was silly before the project began, and just got worse as things progressed.

The problem is that a backlog that looks like a laundry list is very difficult to prioritize. Since the items in them are only barely connected, if at all, they become a challenge to trade off against each other. The stories and items also become difficult to evolve. If the right thing to do for one product goal harms one of the other goals, adjudicating the decision becomes a tough exercise for everyone involved.

It rarely works, but it is possible, for a bottoms-up approach to actually achieve a high-level goal. Once you have gathered enough items on the laundry list, epics and themes may indeed emerge. If that happens, then a second pass needs to be made; once you have themes and epics, all of the other items that don't further the overall goal should be discarded. They may be important and valuable, but they aren't going to help you reach the project goals, so they shouldn't be in the project at all.

Throwing the backlog over the wall. Similarly to the two above, another bad practice is for the product owner to create the entire backlog, then throw it to the team and disengage. The product owner might say that they have a prioritized list of everything they want, and they "trust the team to figure out how to best execute." Despite how this sounds, this actually shows a lack of trust, rather than the opposite.

One of the primary goals is to prevent the "us vs. them" mentality that is all too prevalent in projects and business today. The point of Agile methodologies is to have the development team and the business team work together constantly throughout the project. If the product owner is unwilling to do so, then it spells either a lack of understanding, or a breakdown of trust between the two groups. This usually leads to a disappointing outcome.

One team, many backlogs. Previously, we've discussed strategies for having more than one team operate on the same backlog. You can split the backlog by theme, or you can create a layered product ownership organization, or you can even create separate products or projects. This can sometimes make product owners believe that the opposite is also possible, that you can have one team develop against more than one backlog. Even though this sounds logical, it almost never works.

Even more problematic is that this actually looks good on paper. The development team is fully utilized, progress is being made on all the products, and there is never a time when anyone is idle. In reality, the team lacks alignment, is wasting time by multi-tasking, and their ability to make intelligent decisions is severely lacking.

Once an Agile team has more than one list of priorities to work on, the entire process becomes difficult. The product owner cannot prioritize the entire queue of work, the developers are not entirely sure on what to do next, and the amount of engagement of the team decreases. If the team needs to attend twice as many grooming meetings, planning meetings and retrospective meetings, sooner or later some people will stop coming. While that might make sense from a time utilization standpoint, it will weaken your goals to the point that you might as well stop the product right there.

The only way for this to work is to have each cycle focused on one backlog at a time. This may mean the product owner gets the team for two weeks out of every six, but it is important that each product does get their full attention at some point. History has shown that full attention for a third of the time will yield a better result than a third of their attention all of the time. If you find yourself in this situation, it isn't all bad. Your overall progress will be slowed, but you will have the focus of the team while they are working on your backlog. And you will have more time to groom the backlog, discover new requirements, and digest customer feedback. You just need to make sure that when it's your turn, you do get the team's attention. Splitting their time will hurt everyone.

Chapter 4

Release Planning

One of the primary changes in an Agile environment is the planning horizon. Traditional methods spend a lot of time at the early stages of development attempting to plan out the entire project. Agile methods break up the planning and execution cycles, so that the same amount of planning occurs, but much of it happens while the project is running. But this isn't the only difference. Traditionally, the product owner did the planning, and the team did the development. A critical change in Agile is to let the development team participate in the planning process. This way, the team can not only help make the plan better, but they can feel more engaged and more invested in the plan than they could have felt otherwise.

Release planning thus becomes a collaborative effort, which greatly simplifies the process. Project planning is inherently complicated, which causes the documents and artifacts that try to capture the plan to be complicated as well. Since the development and product teams plan the releases together, the process is much simpler and less mysterious. While the product owner still has final accountability – and final say – on the release plan, the team knows that their input was heard and considered.

Good, Fast, Cheap. Pick Two.

There is an old project management axiom that says of the three attributes: good, fast and cheap, you can only have two in your project. This is sometimes known as the Iron Triangle, or the Project Management Triangle. This is such a ubiquitous chestnut that even though I gave an attempt to source it, I could not. The idea is that you can have good and fast, it will just cost quite a bit. You can have fast and cheap, but it won't be good. Or, you can have good and cheap, but it will take a long time for you to get it.

Agile doesn't have a magic bullet that solves this Iron Triangle. Rather, it casts it aside, and says that's not the right way to look at your project. Agile looks at the three options and says we want all three – but what we can be flexible on is how much functionality we release and how we release it.

Being flexible on the functionality of the product is very aligned with Agile methods in general. As a product owner, you want to begin the project with a clear vision, and some ideas to get started. There is no way for you know everything the product should do before hand, nor should you try. You and the team will be learning about the customer, the market and the product as you go along. Having too long a list of "must haves" is more likely to yield a disappointing product in the end.

Conversely, having a flexible launch date can sometimes lead to a negative customer experience. There have been lots of software packages that were named with a year in the title that didn't actually release in that year. This leads to little more than mockery of the product, and a distrust that it is any good in the first place. My experience is that customers are more accepting of beta versions, even those that contain bugs, than they are of full slips of the release calendar.

Stating your release cadence ahead of time has advantages to the team, as well. The statement of "We are going to launch whatever we have at the end of 90 days" has immense power to focus the team on the MVP, and forces everyone to make difficult choices about what needs to be in the release. Of course, you need to do this responsibly; choosing a release date that is impossible to meet will wind up demotivating your team, and giving you nothing when the time comes.

You should also consider stating a release cadence beyond the first release. If you are going to launch in 90 days, and have a new release every quarter thereafter, you can create a good rhythm with your development team as well as your customers. Everyone will know that improvements come every quarter, but you retain the flexibility to decide what those improvements will be. They could be new features, bug fixes, or better performance. The choice is up to the product owner, but by identifying the release dates, you can create focus on whatever is important to you for that period of time.

Running a project in this manner also has some side benefits when it comes to the management of it. The release cadence becomes natural breaking points to make major decisions, including budgeting, personnel decisions, vacation or holiday leave, and all manners of logistical decisions. With a new cycle coming up in predictable patterns, you are never far away from another decision point when you can decide to stop the project, add or swap team members, spend a few weeks on the beach, or even roll off the product yourself. If you do not have this cadence identified, changes such as these become much more disruptive, and much more difficult for the team to plan.

While it is founded on flexibility, Agile has no flexibility on the subject of quality. While it is easy to say that you will support and create time for quality development, in traditional project methods, those quality items are the first to get cut when time runs short. The solution for this comes in the form of acceptance criteria that are set ahead of time. Quality, which includes not only a well-crafted product, but also documentation, testing support and other controls, are listed in the acceptance criteria of stories, epics and themes. If they aren't completed, then the work isn't done.

As a product owner, you should be very careful about adjusting your acceptance criteria in such a way as to reduce the quality of your product. Cutting out criteria that makes the product more stable or maintainable is not only short-term thinking; it will negatively impact the team and the customer. It is often better to remove entire bits of functionality from a product to gain time, than to cut out quality controls or release an inferior product.

Continuous Delivery

The expectations and difficulty associated with delivering updates to your product have changed drastically in the past two decades. It used to be acceptable to release new versions every few years. Not only were the customers conditioned to only expect improvements infrequently, but the logistics of getting your entire customer base to upgrade added friction to the environment. Many commercial software vendors put policies in place for how many old versions they would support, signaling to their customers that they expect them to not upgrade right away.

The internet has certainly changed the deployment environment. Many applications now look for new updates as their first step before launching, and the notion of getting a new version weekly or even daily is not uncommon. Even major releases are seen as things all users should do as soon as possible, or have the software do for itself. While this is helpful from a deployment perspective, it's also very useful from a product perspective.

Being able to release frequently is a big advantage to product owners. There are many strategies available to get feedback internally; you can set up focus groups, user conferences, do a traveling show where you demo the product, etc. But nothing will give you the type of information that you can get from live customers using the product in live situations. Frequent releases also has the impact of broadening your user base, as you may find that customers that you had never considered are now using your product. The customers will never be able to find your product unless it is in the market; you should strive to get it there as early and as often as possible.

Launching early an often also has another benefit. Your product might entirely miss the mark, or the user base you were hoping to address might not be as large as you thought, or perhaps the price you are setting is too high for your customers. Maybe certain use cases that you thought were critical really are not, and maybe even the entire product is not worth continuing. As long as you are puttering away in private, you won't have to face these questions. But you also won't be releasing a great product.

There is a cost to having continuous releases, of course. Your product must maintain a consistently high quality and new releases must be easy to install. When Apple released a major upgrade to their iOS in 2013, the story hit the evening news as millions of people prepared to have their Apple devices upgrade themselves overnight. Customers woke up with new features and a new UI, but also a few new bugs. The team had to hurry to develop fixes and provide for another release to fix the previous release. But those bugs would never have been found internally, and their commitment to fixing them quickly gained them some leeway for next time.

There is no real strict guideline about how often you should release. This isn't to be confused with the length of a sprint or cycle, this is releasing new functionality to customers. Some companies release weekly, others annually. Most companies have found that planning for a release per quarter – every 90 days – hits the right balance of frequency and stability. Anything longer than a quarter is too long, as you will find you will need to do a non-standard or patch release faster than that. Shorter than a quarter is fine, as long as your team can handle it, but note that you will be spending a lot of time planning and managing the release itself. Balancing speed against the cost of overhead is up to the product owner, but you should err on the side of releasing as often as you can manage.

Key Concepts in Agile

There are a few concepts in Agile methodologies that are different than more traditional methods. If you have an experienced team, they will manage these themselves. However, as a product owner, you must become familiar with the terminology and what they mean. Remember, the product owner is a part of the team, and needs to be as committed to working in an agile fashion as everyone else.

Velocity. For decades, development teams have struggled with the notion of measuring how much work can get done. Teams use time spent, lines of software code written, function points delivered, database actions performed or pages of documentation created as an attempt to answer this question. This is particularly true when a client is paying a consultant to perform work, but it is also true internal to an organization. Sometimes it is even used to determine which team is better than another.

Virtually all of these attempts fail. Development is complicated, and it is often the case that difficult does not necessarily mean valuable. Certain things that are very hard to do might not yield much value, while other fairly easy tasks may make all the difference. It is also the case that there is more than one way for a solution to be made, and if a development team knows that it being measured on something, they may be biased to the solution that the metric most favors.

Knowing how much work a team can do in a given set of time is not only important for evaluative purposes, it is also critical to understand for planning reasons. If the team has more to do this cycle than they have ever successfully done before, then you might have a problem in the near future. If the team is delivering less than they usually have, it can be a sign that something is going wrong that may require your attention. Agile focuses on this need, rather than on determining how good the team is. It uses a metric known as *velocity*.

Velocity is a measure of how many story points a specific team can deliver in a cycle. It is really that simple, and this simplicity makes the metric very useful. Previously, we discussed the notion of story points, and how they are reached through a consensus tool known as Planning Poker. What we didn't discuss was how these stories make into a cycle.

Before each cycle or sprint begins, the team determines how many story points they are willing and able to commit to delivering. This number is based on past history, known events such as vacations, holidays or missing members, as well as overall availability. Story points are then added to the sprint until that number is reached, at which time, no new ones are added. They should be chosen in priority order, and the priorities should not be changed dramatically just to fit more into the release.

For instance, if a team has a velocity of 20, and they already have 18 story points committed to the release, it may be tempting to reach deep into the backlog to find a two point story to include. This is generally a bad idea. The further down the list of priorities you reach, the less likely a story is to be appropriately groomed and ready to be developed. It is also possible that the story was low on the list because it is risky or uncertain. Accelerating it merely because it fits is not a great idea. If you are faced with this situation, you should keep adding stories in priority order, until you run over. If there is only space for a two point story, and the next one on the list is seven points, so be it. Add it anyway. There's a chance that things will work in your favor, and it makes it in. If not, at least the team can begin work on it, making it more likely to be completed in the next cycle.

Velocity scores are specific to a team, and even specific to a sprint. If there are two teams, even if they are working on the same product, they might have a different scale to use for their stories. For instance, you will see a team with a velocity of 100, but none of their stories have point values lower than eight. In other teams, their velocity might be only 20, but they have several one and two point stories in their backlog. It's impossible to compare across teams.

It is possible to compare within the team, however. If you know your average is 30, but you have been only delivering 18 recently, then something may be up. Or maybe you'll find the velocity go up to 45 and stay there for a few sprints. None of this is a sign of anything specific, but it is a sign that you should take a look to see what's going on.

Burndowns. One of the beliefs of Agile practitioners is to remove work that adds little to no value. Most project management and documentation artifacts are viewed using this lens. If it won't add value commensurate with its cost, or if the expense to keep it up to date is too high, then Agile suggests you don't use it. But even the most ardent Agile fanatic agrees that some documentation and planning must be done. Most teams agree that the burndown chart meets the right criteria. It gives the team a sense for how much work has been done, and how much is left – in other words, if they are ahead or behind schedule. And it does so in light enough way that it can be groomed for minutes each day, and kept relevant.

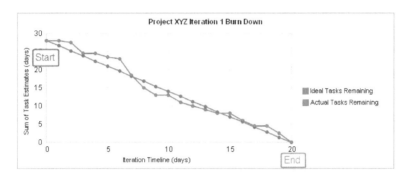

A sample burndown chart.

The purpose of a burndown chart is to track the progress of the team during an iteration. It tracks work completed, work remaining, and time. By viewing all three things at once you can tell at a glance if things are going well, going poorly, or going roughly as expected.

Note that this team is using a four week, or 20 day iteration, and they committed to 28 story points to be completed by the end of the iteration. If a straight line is drawn from on the left, all the way down to 0 on the right, you will find what the ideal progress would be. Then the sum of actual work remaining is tallied each day, and plotted against this ideal. If the actual remaining work is too high above the schedule line and it stays there for too many days in a row, that might be a sign that the team should regroup and replan the sprint.

Note that the artifact can be used not only for sprints, but also for releases or even full product lifecycles. At its heart is the simple tracking of work remaining against time remaining. This can be used for everything that your team is working on; you can have a sprint burndown, a release burndown, and a product burndown, all of which are separate. In fact, there is some value in having one kind of chart that measures everything, as it aids in understanding, and uses less time for people to grasp the message.

Release Planning

Most Agile methodologies don't specifically require a release plan to be made. However, there is an old saying that failing to plan is the same thing as planning to fail. If you don't put together a release plan, it will still happen – teams certainly need to make plans. Some teams find it is okay to use a version of a release burndown instead of a plan. This may work for your team; much of it depends on size and complexity. If your product will be utilizing more than one team at a time, however, this is likely not to provide you with the level of insight and comfort you need.

Sometimes, you will hear teams refer to the release plan as a product roadmap. The idea is that it is a rough set of directions that explain how to get to the final destination that the product owner wants. The release plan is a superset of the release burndown; it contains all the same information, but formatted in a way that isn't mean to guide the day-to-day tasks of the team, but rather as a communication tool for those who are not intimately familiar with the project.

The release plan has four main inputs: (1) Items in the backlog, primarily themes and epics, (2) The velocity of the team, (3) External dependencies and factors, and (4) announced or scheduled releases. Since many of these inputs can change as the product moves forward, the release plan also may need to adjust. Unlike a burndown chart, there is little value in updating it every day; most teams will adjust it at the end of every iteration when new information is known.

At this point, we have all the building blocks to create a plan. We know that stories make up epics, and epics make up themes. We also know that there are sprints or iterations, and there are one or more of them in each release. And we know that in a product's lifespan, it should expect to have several releases. By now you know the length of our iterations, and we know about how much will be developed in each iteration in the form of velocity. It is the release plan that brings all this together into one, top-level view.

Creating the Plan. Once you understand what your team's velocity is, you can start estimating how many sprints your team will need. You should have determined what your Minimal Viable Product is, your MVP, and how many story points it contains. Simple math can tell you that if your MVP requires 100 points, and your team has a velocity of 25, then it will take four iterations for you to reach it.

As product owner, you have the ability to flex some of these numbers. For instance, you can decide to remove acceptance criteria, or even entire themes, from the MVP, in order to reduce the number of story points required. You may also be able to add people or resources to the team, which may have the impact of increasing the team's velocity.

The plan is a basic chart that shows when functionality will be delivered, and when customers will get their hands on it. Note that these are different things; if a release is made up of several sprints, functionality can be delivered well ahead of customer availability. It should be simple enough to fit on a page, and clear enough that customers, stakeholders and the team can understand it. It should be used as a communication tool, rather than a project management one. This will allow you to have the proper conversations with the proper parties, in a way that adds value to the product in the end.

Scaling the Release Plan

Just as we discussed the concept of Chief Product Owners and things like a Scrum of Scrums, there are times when the product we are working on is so large that we need different tools to create the plan. One of the things to keep in mind when scaling any Agile practice is to remain true to the core principles. Those include valuing people and relationships, working software over documentation, and the value of ownership. Adding new processes that break these rules turn your project from being agile to being something developers like to derisively call "fragile." Here are some practices you need to follow if you own a particularly large product.

Planning Consistency. If your project is big enough that you have multiple development teams actively working and planning, then it is critical that you gain some consistency in how the planning is performed. In particular, it is important that the values and estimates being used in any planning poker exercise are the same. While each team will still be expected to have their own velocity, keeping the effort evaluations on the same scale will avoid problems that are only visible from the top level of the project.

For instance, if all of the items in the overall backlog are being estimated using a different scale, then it becomes impossible for the product owner to know how much overall effort remains in the product. It also makes it a challenge to move an item from one team's backlog to the other. Team autonomy is important, and each team should be given the freedom to estimate for themselves, but it is important that everyone is speaking the same language.

Usually, if the product team started small and grew into adding teams along the way, then this is done on its own. The teams already have a history of estimating and they have a pattern to follow for what items of certain sizes should be given. But if the product begins with several teams, making sure that everyone is working off the same set of assumptions should be managed actively. This can be done by having a few people from each team get together every so often to calibrate their estimates, or even by having everyone from all the teams get together to talk about items in the backlog. Even a combination of both might work.

Outlook Horizon. If you are the Chief Product Owner and responsible for planning across several teams, then you have two layers of planning that needs to happen. First, each team will have their own levels of plans, based on what they deem to be priorities and what that team needs to accomplish. While this is likely to produce good results at the team level, as CPO, you are more concerned with producing optimal results across all teams.

This means that each team needs to expand their horizon for backlog grooming. Rather than having this iteration fully groomed and working on the next one, they will need to have two or three sprints mostly groomed, and continuing to look forward. Product owners now not only have to be responsible for their own teams, but also in communicating things to other teams, as early as possible.

It could be that one team contains a pre-requisite for another, or that two teams will want to work in the same area of the product at the same time. Perhaps there is some resource that more than one team needs, but they cannot use it at the same time. This kind of roadblock is easier to see and easier to resolve when it is all within one team. Once teams need to depend on each other, extra care needs to be taken to ensure smooth delivery.

It is also important for the CPO to examine the team sizes. It's possible that one team is overburdened, or underutilized, which means that you should rebalance the teams. This can be done either by moving people from one team to another, or by moving backlog items. Depending on the situation, it may be easier to do one over the other. Any change of this type will cause the individual team to replan, and they should be given the freedom to do so. But it is the CPO's job to ensure the best outcome for all teams.

Reclassifying teams. I struggled if this belonged in this section or the next section as a worst practice. If you are building a large enough product, you may be tempted to utilize some teams developing functionality for customer use, and other teams building infrastructure or internal components. That is one team will be a supplier and another will be a consumer. This can work, but it creates a lot of management needs, and can create team conflict, which is what we are trying to avoid in the first place.

One of the key components of Agile is to allow for each team to set their own priorities. If one team is depending on another to be able to get their work completed, then a conflict is created. Either the team sets their backlog priority based on the needs of another team, or they set their list of priorities based on their own needs. Each method is fraught with peril.

It certainly can be done, but it needs more management from the CPO and the product owners than other methods. When a team decides for itself what to commit to getting done, they feel invested and they understand what they are doing. In this situation, they are working one something that was externally prioritized, even though it all leads into the same product. This means that more communication and more alignment is needed in order to keep things running properly. If you attempt to try this kind of setup, be aware that it may take more of your time than you are able to give.

Anti-Patterns in Planning

People new to Agile planning often struggle with grasping the concepts. Additionally, people who are skilled and experienced at other types of planning tend to fall back on doing what they know, even if those things are not right for the situation they find themselves in. Planning in an agile environment takes a change both to what the plan itself looks like, and the mindset of those doing the planning.

Bottoms-up release planning. Many product owners feel liberated by the notion of not creating large plans. This is especially true of product owners who were once responsible for creating massive, multi-year plans that took hundreds of pages to detail. It is easy for a new agile product owner to think that all they really need to detail out is the next iteration, and perhaps start thinking about the one after that. After all, they think, the plan is subject to change.

This is almost certain to lead to disaster. When you examine a list of backlog items they all tend to look important. In fact, they are all important, otherwise they would not be on the backlog in the first place. What you need to have is a firm understanding of what needs to be done *first*, and not just what needs to be done at all. Determining a priority order cannot be done by looking at the items; it needs to be done by looking at the epics and themes, and how the relate to the release plan.

It is the release plan – the vision for what will be in the next (or first) release of the product – that will drive prioritization. If an item does not further the goal of being ready for a release, then the item should not get worked on at this point in the project. You need to understand the plan, or your prioritization will be incomplete.

Additionally, without a release plan, it is virtually impossible to track progress accurately. A product that has five themes that are each 60% complete is much less ready for launch than one that has two themes that are finished, even though less work has been done. Not having a release plan, or creating one bottoms-up using your backlog items, will lead the team astray.

Passive Product Ownership. As mentioned earlier, the product owner is a full and active member of the team. This isn't meant to be a cliché, such as "we're all one team here." This is meant to be one of the primary changes that Agile proposes to the overall relationship. If the product owner does not take a driving role in the project, then it will quickly devolve into a traditional-looking arrangement that will harm both the team and the product.

You will sometimes see new product owners attempt to delegate certain tasks to the team, the project manager or ScrumMaster. This can be especially true when the team is more experienced with Agile than the product owner or if the product owner is especially busy. In fact, the team may even offer to take some of the responsibilities of the product owner, in an attempt to relieve pressure. It won't work out.

The product owner must be an active force in every activity. This includes release planning, backlog grooming, iteration planning and retrospectives. Only the product owner can decide the item acceptance criteria, prioritize items, and decide when a product is ready for release. If the product owner is not active with the team, the team will either operate under "best guess" or it will damage the relationship between the team and the product owner. Not being a full participant brings back the "us vs. them" situation that is the entire point in the first place.

Waiting for the perfect. There are two aspects to Agile development that can be scary to a product owner. The first is that the needs of the market are unknown and unknowable. No matter how smart a product owner may be, or the amount of research and analysis that is performed, there is no way to be certain how the market will react to a product. The second is that more products fail than succeed. Products that are not quite right for the need, or that missed the window of opportunity or that are simply wrong, are more common than the opposite.

Both of these concepts can be unsettling even to the most experienced product owner. This can cause the product owner to continually hold off on a release, awaiting one more focus group, or one more quarter, or for one more feature to be developed. In other words, the product launch is delayed, sometimes continually.

Agile doesn't make product owners smarter, or give them better foresight. The two problems above, unknowable market needs and high risk of failure, still exist. What Agile methodologies do is recognize them as realities, and figure out how to use them to the team's advantage. This is done through releasing early and often.

Waiting for the perfect time to release will cause you to miss out on customer feedback, prevent the team from changing course, and will have you relying upon information from somewhere other than a "live" environment. Additionally, it could be you are working on a product that no one wants at all – or maybe it appeals to a market segment that you had not expected – and you will never know it without putting your product in the market. Early and often should be your primary focus; don't fear failure, just don't delay it.

Chapter 5

Directing the Team

People who first hear of Agile methodologies think it sounds like chaos. No documentation, no meetings, no command and control. It proposes self-organizing teams, no management, and little oversight committees. How can anything meaningful get done in this kind of environment? Won't it be a lot of people running around with no one making sure progress is being made in the right direction? Where are my TPS reports?

I wish that last question was a joke. Many organizations require utility-free (i.e., useless) documentation, reports and meetings as a way to keep control of a project. What these organization rarely realize is that by forcing the team to perform all these low-value tasks, they are pulling them away from working on making the product better. Even worse, it will have the effect of stifling the creativity and flexibility of the team, causing it to be less agile.

Upon a closer look, someone who understands how Agile is meant to work finds that the methodology does something clever. One thing that project managers that are new to an organization tend to do is to look at the full list of documents, meetings and artifacts they are expected to produce. Sometimes they will remove a few or combine a few, but for the most part, they use the existing structure as the baseline, and attempt to only make incremental changes.

Agile took the other direction. All project work should be in support of one of three key needs: Alignment, Planning and Adjusting. There are things built into the process that do everything needed for those three needs, and only those three needs. All other activities, even those meant to provide comfort to stakeholders and managers, are cast aside.

This slimmed down what a product owner needed to manage, but put even more emphasis on making sure that those things were done thoroughly. In a traditional process, where you are making dozens of documents that you suspect no one will read, you don't necessarily take the most care in making sure they are done consistently and correctly. Agile removes most of the work, but falls apart if they aren't done diligently.

There are six main activities that will drive your Agile team. The product owner must be an active participant in all of them. Let's take a look at what they are, and how a product owner should be participating in them.

Iteration Planning. At the beginning of each iteration, the team should gather to choose the work they are going to accomplish, and to commit to achieving the goal for the iteration. Some teams will erroneously say that iteration planning happens "between" iterations. That is not the right way to look at it; planning the iteration is actually the beginning of the cycle. It is as important to the success as actually doing the work.

The product owner's role during this discussion is to clarify what the goals and requirements are. This can mean answering questions, clarifying needs, expressing the overall goal of the iteration and how it fits into the release plan, and other topics that provide information to the team. It is up to the team to determine what will actually get done, and how it will get done. The product owner is not allowed to tell the team how much work they should commit to, nor should you ask for a specific solution or design. This is a partnership, but the product owner owns the requirements, and the team owns the implementation. Without those boundaries, the team cannot make personal commitments for what they will accomplish, which is a necessary ingredient for success.

One of the goals of Agile development is to keep your team at a pace that is sustainable for the long term. Planning actually depends upon it. If the team tries to be over-ambitious, or attempt to reach unrealistic goals, not only will it impact the current cycle, but it will impact all future planning cycles. Agile relies upon a smooth, predictable amount of story points being developed in each cycle, and a steady stream of work flowing from the backlog into completed status.

Reaching commitments and achieving a degree of predictability is valued more than over-achievement. Not only do you run the risk of burning the team, but putting the screws to everyone in an effort to get a little more work also will stifle their creativity and their ability to contribute to the product.

Agile calls the amount of work the team signs up to complete as a commitment, which means that the team will use all of their best efforts to reach it. When it comes to development, nothing is ever totally certain. Things can come up, items can turn out to be harder than expected, or the team can be new or can have new members who haven't quite calibrated how much they can get done. While disappointing, this happens. Later on, we will discuss iteration retrospectives, and how they can be used to open the discussion to prevent it from happening too frequently.

Defining Done. Agile methodologies have a concept called the "Definition of Done." This is a key concept to understand as a product owner. In traditional project management, much time and energy is spent trying to determine how complete something is. Trying to parse the difference between something being 55% complete or 62% is not only not worth discussion, but it also adds no value to the project. In Agile, something is either done, or it isn't. There is no gradient.

Because of this, it is vital for the team to understand what it means for an item to be declared done. This is done by having the product owner describe the criteria that must be true in order for it to be complete. This includes not only functioning as expected, in all respects, but also that it is documented, tested and ready for the release.

Items have acceptance criteria and permanent criteria. The acceptance criteria are entirely within the control of the product owner. These are the things that the story must *do* in order to be complete. The permanent criteria are created through agreement of the entire team, and include the things that the story must *be* in order to put it into the done column. This includes documented, training created, unit tests running, and any other thing that the team agrees should be done for all items.

Once the permanent criteria are established, the product owner should never request that they are changed. A consistent set of quality controls is critical for the health of both the team and the product. If they aren't done, then neither is the backlog item. It's that simple.

Daily standup meetings. Most flavors of Agile contain a very short, daily meeting. These meetings are alternately called a daily standup, or a daily scrum, or even a roll call meeting. The product owner should make it a habit to attend these meetings; remember, the product owner is a full and active member of the team.

But more than just participating, the product owner can learn a lot about the progress of the project and where it might need help from these daily discussions. The development team will be talking about what they did yesterday, what they are doing today, and what (if anything) is currently in their way. As product owner, you want to listen to the progress being made, so that you can gauge the speed at which things are moving. You also want to listen for impediments that the team identifies; often the product owner is able to help clear them or clarify the needs to get the team moving again.

You should   be prepared to share any information that you have about the product, or customer research, or just new data that you have. The team is generally focused on the tasks at hand, so any insight they can get into the rest of the product is often most welcome. Finally, you should be ready to talk about what you are doing next. That could be doing more backlog grooming, or visiting a customer site, or sending out a survey, or any number of things you would expect a product owner to be doing. The team will want to know what you are up to, and this is the right forum to let them know.

While you do want to fully participate, you need to be careful not to interfere. Agile teams like to organize themselves, often creating leadership and reviewer roles organically. It is important that you don't attempt to assign tasks to people, nor express any frustration at the progress being made. If you are uncomfortable with the way things are going, this isn't the forum to highlight it. You can ask the team how they are feeling, and if they still feel they'll hit the goal for the iteration. At this point, however, everything is in motion, so unless the answers are highly negative, you should still find a more productive meeting to bring up the topic.

Backlog grooming. The backlog is the primary artifact used for managing the project. At its core, it is just a prioritized list of things to be worked on, and can be as simple as a whiteboard or sticky notes, or can be done in a fancy software tool. Because it is so vital to the project, the product owner not only needs to pay meaningful attention to it, the team needs to be involved as well. This act is called backlog grooming.

There are three main tasks that are all within the responsibilities of the product owner. They are: creating or removing items, clarifying existing items, and setting priorities on those items. As much as possible, these tasks should be done in full view of the team. While it is helpful for the product owner to do a lot of the work independently, the team will want to see some of the outcome and understand the reasoning behind it.

The product owner is the only person who is authorized to add or remove an item from the backlog. This is intentional. If too many people have the ability to add items, then you wind up with more than one list, your stuff and other people's stuff. If someone outside of the team wants something that isn't on the list, you either need to adopt it and make it your own, or you need to let the person know that their item isn't going to make the list. The team will appreciate knowing who has the final say on what is in and what is out.

Clarifying existing items is where the true grooming comes into play. Most of the items on the backlog will be too big or too vague or too unfinished to be ready to be worked upon. They need to be broken down, expanded upon, and have their acceptance criteria and definition of done created. As often as possible, this should be done live with the team. The team will be of great value in assisting breaking large tasks into smaller ones, and they will have questions that are highly valuable to ask at this point in the process. This is also a time when the team can describe to you the cost of some of the acceptance criteria, which will allow you to think about how many points a story is worth, and how strict you want to be on it.

Some teams perform backlog grooming a little bit each day. Others will do it once a week or once an iteration. There is not magic recipe for how often to do it, other than to say that it must be done, and it should be done as a collaboration between the product owner and the project team.

Similar to grooming and clarifying is prioritizing. Once items have been fully described, they still need to be put in priority order in the backlog. This too should be done with the team. The team can not only help sharpen the focus on what is important and what is not, but they will want to know the product owner's rationale behind what the priorities are. The more open you are as a product owner, the more likely the team will adapt to your needs, and act accordingly. The more you try to force priorities without description, the more pushback you should expect from the team.

Review meeting. One of the features of Agile is the desire for transparency and frequent checkpoints. One way this is achieved is through review meetings. This meeting happens as the end of every iteration, and just like planning, is considered to be a part of the cycle. If the review hasn't been held, then the iteration isn't complete.

The goal of the meeting is to review the actual progress to date by actually looking at whatever has been built. There is little concept of a "stoplight dashboard" in Agile, where a project manager continually calls their project "green" even while it is running directly off the rails. Agile is very non-judgmental about how things got to be the way they are, the only goal is to openly understand the current state, and to adjust if necessary.

The review meeting can contain anyone the product owner wants to invite. This can be customers, users, members of sales or service, executives or even the press. The only constant is that the product owner must be at each one. No matter who is invited, the meeting should be matter-of-fact, and not a dog-and-pony show. This isn't a demo, nor is it a pitch meeting. It is simply a review of work done to date, to look at what is ready to be accepted. The goal of the project is to create transparency, not to make sales.

The product owner's role is to get the ball rolling, explain the goal of the iteration, and show how what was actually accomplished helped further this goal. Each backlog item that was produced should be tested thoroughly against the acceptance criteria, and only those that fully pass all tests should be accepted. Those items that are lacking should get put back on the backlog with notes about what needs to be changed. Agile has no concept of "partially complete;" either an item is ready, or it is not. There is no real harm in putting something incomplete on the backlog; there is real harm in accepting something as done which is not.

As product owner, you need to be sure to respect the work done, while remaining honest about progress towards the release goal. If the team made a lot of progress this iteration, you should make sure to mention it. If the team struggled, or didn't get as much done as hoped, you should say that as well. Remember, you are a full member of the team, so failure to meet the goal is also your responsibility. Don't point fingers at individuals; be sure to include yourself as part of the team.

Once you have completed the assessment of the work completed in the sprint, you should start asking for feedback. This can come from stakeholders, customers, the team, or anyone who happens to be in the room with you. Ask if they like what was done, if anyone thinks changes are necessary, and if the vision that the product is trying to reach is still a good one. Ask what functionality is obviously missing, or if there are things that are developed that aren't all that important and should be cut out.

During these meetings, new requirements and stories tend to get generated. Once people can see the product taking form, they start to realize things they forgot about, or didn't realize in the first place. Don't judge the requests now, just capture them. New stories, epics and themes will need to be groomed and prioritized before you can decide if they will be included in the final product. Respect the audience by attempting to faithfully capture the request, and considering it later in the project.

Retrospective meetings. One of the more interesting aspects of the Agile movement is the notion that the movement might not be entirely correct. Just as in product development, the needs of the users and the requirements of the product aren't knowable before people start to use it. Most Agile frameworks build in some time to reflect on the entire process using something called a retrospective.

This meeting should occur every iteration, and it is not focused on the product or the project, it is focused on the team and how things are being done. Each development cycle should be better than the one before, and not just because the team is expected to improve. Every time through the cycle, the team will be expecting to make changes that will make them more effective, and just about everything is on the table. Ideas can range from trying out a new technical architecture to setting the thermostat higher or lower by two degrees. Everything will and should be discussed, as anything that makes the team better should be considered.

As product owner, you should attend these meetings, too. Sometimes, these meetings are combined with the review meeting, but they don't have to be. Some of the needed improvements might actually be in your own performance, and the team won't be shy in letting you know. Other things will need to be discussed and ideas generated, and you want to make sure that you are there to be a participant in that discussion.

Making continuous improvement to the team is a difficult task, and it requires willingness and an openness to change. It also requires that team members need to be willing to admit they are wrong, or that they could do something better. If it is as simple as using larger sticky notes on the wall, then some of the ideas can be implemented immediately. If the ideas will take time to develop and produce, they should be added to the product backlog and prioritized.

Agile is very reflective, but it is also flexible. It can be used to make itself better, once more is learned about the environment. And each item should be considered, placed on the backlog, groomed and prioritized appropriately. It is important that there is only one list of things to do, no matter how diverse that list may be.

Scaling up meetings

In previous chapters we have discussed how to use these strategies with larger and larger projects. As you work with Agile, you'll find the process to be very scalable and a lot of the same constructs and artifacts are used. However, some of the tasks need to be modified or altered in order to properly support a larger effort. The basic idea is still the same, but a little more caution and care need to be invested to keep all the teams aligned and everyone headed towards the same goal.

Scaling Iteration Planning. If you have several teams all working in concert, you will likely find yourself holding a large planning meeting that contains members from all of the teams. This is going to cause you to perform some additional work up front, including grooming more backlog than normal, doing more joint estimating and sizing, and aligning with other product owners.

Previously, we discussed that a product owner can usually handle two teams, or one team if they are also acting a chief product owner. Therefore, if your project has more than two teams, it should have more than one product owner. Ensuring alignment with all the product owners and all the teams is vital to success.

Each team will continue to do their own iteration planning as normal, working on whatever the highest priority items in their backlog is at the time. Once this is done, all of the plans should be put together, to see what the entire project intends to complete by the end of the iteration. With a very large project, you will want to take a look at each team individually as well as the "view from the top" to make sure that the right things are happening.

Scrum of Scrum, or Stand-up of Stand-ups. Agile works best when the team is in constant contact. This ensures that the teams cannot get too far astray from the goals or from each other. The daily stand-up is one mechanism suggested to keep this alignment. But with several teams, having everyone stand around and give even a 30 second update isn't feasible. Not only will it take too long, but it's unlikely that the value created is worth the effort.

The teams do need to coordinate with each other, and often on a daily basis. They should be discussion work completed, work planned, items at risk, and more importantly any dependencies the teams have on each other or impediments they are experiencing. Many teams meet this need through the concept of a stand-up of stand-ups.

After the daily meeting of the teams, each team then sends representatives to another daily meeting. Just as in the smaller meeting, each person is afforded about a minute to discuss progress and talk about issues or other topics that are of interest to the day. Sometimes, it is the product owner who is the representative, but it can also be a developer or the project manager. The product owners, and in particular, the chief product owner, should attend this meeting as often as possible, keeping in mind that the same rules apply about how to participate.

Revue of Reviews. Similar to the stand-up of stand-ups, each team should proceed with their review meetings as normal. Acceptance criteria should be tested, users and customers invited, and stakeholders consulted. Any tactical changes, such as putting items back on the backlog, or discovering new requirements should still happen in the team review meeting.

If you are working with multiple teams, you will want to see what the other teams have completed, ask questions and provide feedback yourself. One way to do this would be to have a large auditorium, invite every stakeholder, and give a series of presentations. This tends to be impractical, as it could take all day and a very large room, just to get through the material. Additionally, it sets the wrong tone for the project. Agile believes that there is power in collaboration and two-way communication, not in lecture hall style presentations. If you have a huge audience, or you just want to present to customers and gather feedback a different way, then this might be your only choice.

Many companies find that approach will yield unsatisfying results. It is difficult to get the right level of excitement and engagement from the audience, especially on a repeated basis. The people whom you are trying to interact with won't feel the same level of personal attention, and will begin to suspect that no one would notice if they didn't attend. And eventually, some of them will stop attending.

Other industries have solved this problem before, using trade shows, career fairs, or even dog expositions for example. Since the goal is to get high-quality, engaged feedback, and to interact with the stakeholder base, then trying to do so from a podium in an auditorium is beyond most people's ability.

Setting up several "booths" where the stakeholders can wander from one to the next, or even setting up 20 minute "rotations" can allow for two things. First, all the stakeholders can spend as much time as they want with any team. If they have a particular interest, or if they have deep questions, they can make sure that their needs are satisfied and their voices heard. Second, the team is forced to give their demonstrations multiple times, and perhaps answer the same questions repeatedly. While this sounds inefficient, it is actually a very effective way to gather feedback. If the team meets with eight groups in the course of the "expo" and six of them all ask the same question, then the team knows it has more work to do on that topic. Also, by demonstrating their work over and over again, not only do they get to have a sense of pride in what they've accomplished, but they also continue to learn more and more about their own product. There are a lot of benefits to holding reviews in this fashion.

Group Retrospectives. The last item in every iteration is to hold a retrospective. This meeting is intended not to examine the product, but the process. What is working well and should be continued, what isn't working so well and should be changed, and what external forces need to be managed for next time. This is a vital part of the process, one that uses Agile methods to improve on your ability to be agile.

Once you have multiple teams, scaling this process in an effective way is difficult. The retrospective requires the honesty of the team, a first-hand understanding of the issues or successes, and the creativity of everyone to help come up with solutions. The same strategy as the stand-up of stand-ups can be used, and representatives from each team can come together to discuss what each team said, but experience says this doesn't give good results. Unless the teams have been working together for a very long time, and have a deep trust in each other, and are working in the same space and can understand the issues, the conversation will stall.

I have seen companies try to handle this challenge in several ways, none of them are perfect. One way is to hold a full retrospective, with all team members, on some regular cadence. If your project is running on one-month cycles, for instance, you can hold an all-hands retrospective every quarter. Here you can discuss what was said at the team level retrospectives for the last three iterations, and generate discussion with everyone involved.

Often this type of meeting can be combined with other all-hands type activities, and it can be made into a half-day or full day meeting. If your teams don't work in the same building, this can be a way to get the team together so that they can build relationships with each other, as well as discussing progress on the product and doing retrospectives.

Another approach is to organize retrospectives around topics. Again, each team continues to do their own retrospective, taking actions as needed for their own team. From these meetings, themes will emerge that affect the whole project or are cross-team in nature. These topics can be rolled up and then new meetings can emerge among them.

For instance, you might find that all the teams are uncomfortable with the facilities, want crisper graphic art done, and really like working with some new technology. Rather than have a meeting where all three topics are discussed, you can create topic-based group retrospectives around each of the topics. Those that are interested or motivated by any topic can attend one or all of them, so that they can be engaged in the discussion and help craft solutions. This is also a good way for team members who don't work directly with each other to build relationships.

Anti-Patterns in Team Management

The product owner is not only responsible for managing the product backlog and directing the team. The role also has the responsibility of setting the tone and attitude of the teams and the project. The development team will be excited to have the product owner as a fully engaged member of the team, and they are ready to take some direction. But if they catch any sense of the "Us vs. Them" mentality, or a product owner who doesn't seem interested in collaboration, then you will wind up with the worst outcome – an agile team that isn't working together. Here are some things to avoid.

Product owner as customer. There is a big difference between acting like a member of the team, and acting like a customer. Customers tend to want to be impressed, feel like they need to be sold or convinced, and at the end, think they can simply walk away and not buy anything. This is a terrible way to be a product owner.

A product owner who acts like a customer will be involved in writing requirements and again at reviews, but probably not in between. They will let the team know what they want, and then wait until it is done to see if they still want it. Sometimes they will even do this on purpose, making themselves hard to find or difficult to reach. This way, if the team does the wrong thing, the product owner feels justified in placing the blame elsewhere.

Agile doesn't work without a product owner, so this means someone will step up to fill the void. This is often the project manager or ScrumMaster, and it lets the team be productive, but it is no substitute for having the product owner feel like a member of the team, and to be the one making the decisions.

An active and committed product owner is critical to the success of an Agile product. Your involvement is what makes Agile different from other methodologies, and it should be your top priority. If you act like a customer, the product may fail, and it will be your fault.

Accepting vapor. There is a whole concept in software development called "vaporware." It is usually used for products that are announced or rumored to be released that never make it to market. The demos usually exist, and a sales engineer can walk you through it and comment about features that either barely exist or will be in a future release. And while you may even contract to buy it, the product will never be delivered.

In projects, it is easy to get tricked by demos, PowerPoint slides, and prototypes. Your mind will be convinced that even though the functionality doesn't totally exist, that it is very close to being ready. Depending on the presenter, they may even be very convincing, and leave you with the feeling that the product is right there, ready for you to use. But it's not.

Agile stresses avoiding this. The sprint review should show real software running in an environment that isn't development. All of the criteria for "done" need to be met, and need to be shown. This should be done even if customers or executives are there to see it – if the acceptance criteria has been met, then it should be proven. If it hasn't then it should go back on the backlog. There is very little wiggle room. If it's not done, it's not done. End of story.

The hot and cold product owner. The hot and cold product owner is very similar to the product owner who thinks like a customer. Sometimes, they are very excited and interested in the product, and other times they are the opposite. They will alternate between praising the team and criticizing the progress. Even direct questions won't give actionable answers, and the team won't know from day to day if they are going to get the hot treatment, or the cold shoulder.

This can happen even if the product owner is engaged with the team. They can be attending daily meetings, grooming the backlog, participating in retrospectives, and performing all of the duties that a good product owner should. But they don't feel like part of the team; they feel like being full of praise one day and criticism the next is a way to motivate, just like you would employees.

By all means, if there is something bad going on, it is fair to be critical. And it's fine to praise something that's going well. But the product owner cannot be fickle, and some days decide to be nice and other times a tyrant. While the product owner is ultimately responsible for the delivery, they also must maintain the status as good teammate. If you aren't, you may find your team stops inviting you to meetings.

The "gimme more" product owner. There are two seemingly conflicting principles in Agile. The first states that "Agile processes promote sustainable development. The sponsors, developers, and users should be able to maintain a constant pace indefinitely."[7] The second is that there are no breaks between iterations. This is no built in recovery time, no down time, etc. Even the planning and retrospectives are done during the development cycle. So, how to you keep a team running at full speed without allowing them to take a break?

The answer to this comes in allowing the team themselves to decide how much work they are going to commit to in a

---

[7] This is right from the Agile Manifesto

given iteration. The team must have the ability to make sure that their workload is sustainable and realistic and that they don't burn themselves out.

One of the worst situations for this is a product owner who feels like a demanding client, always wanting more. By consistently asking for more than can be delivered, the product owner may get more done – for a time. But it won't work longer term, and may not even work more than once. But that doesn't stop bad product owners from trying it.

If you consistently request more work than can be done, the team will eventually burn out, get sick, take a lot of vacation, or leave altogether. You simply must understand the team is the one making the decision on how much can be done in the given time, and you must abide by their decision. If you aren't comfortable with the amount of output, you should bring it up in the retrospective, but you cannot and should not force the team to go at a pace they aren't comfortable with. You won't keep your team very long if you do this.

Process abuse. There are organizations that either don't trust or don't understand that Agile has components that cover all the needs of a project. What you will sometimes see is all the correct artifacts, being used in all the wrong ways. As is usually the case, this gives the worst of all possible outcomes, as no one really knows what is going on, and the artifacts are all being used incorrectly.

This tends to be done because someone wants to run the project in a traditional way, and use old control mechanisms. For instance, the burndown chart will talk about items being done, or not done. There is no real concept of partial credit. Traditional methods not only allow for partially completed items, they practically thrive on it. If you are using your burndown chart as a way to say that you are "81% complete" with your work – even though nothing is actually complete – then you are abusing the process.

It may also be that someone outside the product or a key stakeholder is requesting tighter control on a project, and the existing artifacts are being repurposed. This isn't as bad, but it still points to a complete lack of trust in the team and the process. If more visibility is needed, there are ways to do that. Invite the stakeholder to more reviews and retrospectives, shorten the iteration times to allow for more frequent updates, or focus on the release plan (not the iteration plan) as a means to discuss what will be ready for customers. Resist the urge to use the process in the wrong way; it will wind up pleasing no one.

Chapter 6

How to become a great product owner

My initial draft of this book did not include this chapter. The first five sections of this book are about what a product owner does, and how to do it. As I began discussing the content of this book, virtually everyone asked a question that I hadn't considered – "How does someone become a great product owner?" Depending on your organization's adoption of Agile, you may be the first product owner in your company, without much guidance or people to learn from. Your team may be new at it as well, meaning no one knows what to expect. This is both a blessing and a curse.

Growing Yourself

If you are new at being a product owner, or if you think you might want to be one, you should take responsibility of growing yourself into the role. This is a different kind of role than others you may have played before, and a good product owner's career potential is virtually limitless. Some of the best and most innovative CEOs in recent times either started or simply acted like product owners. Deciding what to work on, what to accept, and when to launch are all duties of product owners and CEOs alike. It also probably means that no one is fully qualified for the job before they get started.

Understand your weaknesses. The role of product owner requires skills in virtually all areas. You need to be inspiring and able to motivate the team, you need to talk with customers and stakeholders, do research and analysis, be decisive yet willing to adapt, and most of all, you need to be ready to accept that you are the final word on everything. It's a big job.

It's unlikely that you majored in product ownership in university, so you will be looking to learn by doing, as well as by getting training. The Scrum Alliance offers training on how to be a product owner, as well as how to be a ScrumMaster and a team member. If feasible, you should consider taking all of them. Learning not only what is expected of you, but what is expected of everyone will greatly enhance your understanding of the process.

While training is helpful, nothing will prepare you better than actually doing the job. You should focus on living the Agile values of being committed, being honest and transparent, valuing relationships, and have the strength to do the right thing by the team and the product. For the most part, living the values will get you further down the track than any training will.

You should also be ready to make some mistakes. Most people are new at this and should be expected to do some things wrong the first time around. If you are respectful and honest, your team will not only forgive you, but they will welcome the opportunity for you to improve. They should be as committed to the Agile movement as you are, and it is in everyone's best interest for you to get better.

Finally, don't be afraid to ask. The retrospective meetings were put into the methodology specifically for this need. It is a time to ask about team effectiveness, what can be better, and what is already good. You should also be asking the team for feedback on your performance, and where you can improve. Inspect and adapt, are keys to the continuous improvement cycle in Agile; it doesn't just go for the product, it goes for the team and the product owner, as well.

Live the values. No matter how new or experienced you are the job, living the core values will be something that sets you apart from others. Agile values respect, truth, transparency, trust and commitment. As product owner, you must live these values yourself if you have any hope of fostering them in your team.

These values sound trite and commonplace, but experience shows that they are not. Many teams have been conditioned to avoid one or all of the five core values due to negative outcomes in the past, either personally or to the project. Truth tends to be the first one to suffer, as people learn to "go along to get along." While this might make for less destructive relationships and might prolong people's employment, it makes for a mediocre product.

Agile relies upon frequent and constant Inspect-and-Adapt activities, where the current state of the product, team, project, and product owner are all evaluated. If change is needed – or even if you want to try something out – it will require trust, transparency and truth. If team members are afraid to say what they think and feel, then they won't be involved in generating new ideas. And it may be these ideas that make your product great.

One of the ways that Agile suggests to help with this is to create the environment where behaviors that support the values can be displayed. Positive conflict needs to be created, so that the process can be improved and innovation has the chance to be surfaced. If the environment discourages conflict, then not only will you not have a forum by which to live the values, but you will also miss out on all the creativity that comes as a result.

The final value, commitment, is the one that the product owner should be most concerned with. It's easy to say that you are committed to the success of the product, but it is much harder to live that statement. The product owner cannot blame the team for any failure; the product owner is a member of that team. Making everyone feel accountable for all phases of the product will make a difference in the overall success of the effort.

Get support from everywhere. If this is your first time as a product owner, or even if it isn't, you are going to need as much support as you can find. This includes the support from the team, support from your sponsors, and even support from outside the team. It's possible to be successful without the support of all of these three groups, but your life will be much easier if you are able to seek it out and obtain it.

Support from the team should be the most obvious, but it is easy to overlook. The team wants you and the product to succeed, remember, you are on the team yourself. But there is a tendency for new product owners to disguise their weaknesses or their inexperience, and hope to fake confidence in order to win over their team. This is usually the worst avenue to take. If you have an experienced team, they will be willing and able to help set expectations, evaluate and help you course correct, and even give you strategies to use. The way to gain the support of the team is by being truthful and transparent, and living the core values.

Gaining support of your sponsors is also critical. To be effective, you need the trust from your executive chain, and they must understand what the role of product owner entails. This may even require you to help teach them about the role and how they can help. The primary thing you want from your management is authority and autonomy. The methodology works when it is the team that has final say on how things are done, and the product owner who has final say on what gets done. As soon as either side feels they can escalate to undermine a decision, the whole system falls apart. Ensuring that everyone is going to support each other is one of the key success factors for any Agile effort.

Many Agile practitioners have also found a meaningful benefit from having an outside expert as a mentor or coach. The coach can help in understanding how to be more effective within the framework of the methodology, as well as a sounding board for feedback or changes. If things start to go wrong, it can be this outside influence that helps get them back on track. They can also help with training specific areas of weakness that you may have, using live details from the project that is running. You may find that you do just fine without a coach, but even very experienced product owners derive benefit from having someone play the role for them.

Keep Growing. Once you have gone through a few iterations, or even launched a few products, it can be easy for you to think that you now know all there is to know about being a product owner. What you will find is that Agile is constantly changing, and it is doing so on purpose. Each team you work with will have different norms and styles, and each product will have different challenges. And along the way, the Agile landscape will continue to drift as new best practices are discovered and discussed.

It is not safe to assume that something that worked very well with one team on one product will work well on another. Indeed, this may even frustrate you as a product owner, as you need to abandon a practice that was very successful in one situation, but isn't in your current one. The only way to find this out is to continue to use the inspect-and-adapt strategy on everything, including your own performance.

In the past decade, many new artifacts, needs and tactics have been uncovered when it comes to running an Agile product. You need to remain aware of things that other organizations are finding helpful, to evaluate if you want to try them out yourself. While true, just because one group finds something valuable doesn't mean that yours will, you need to remain open to trying it out so that you can see for yourself. Keep your abilities growing, and remain open to getting better, and your end result is likely to improve.

Growing Others

At some point, you may find yourself as the most experienced product owner in your group. Perhaps you are acting a CPO, or perhaps you are managing other product owners. Doing so is a challenging balance; you must empower the product owners you are trying to lead, but you must also guide them into becoming better at their craft. Having enough experienced and capable product owners might make the different between successful Agile adoption in your organization and failure.

Properly value the role. The product owner is meant to have final say on everything having to do with the product. Even if you directly manage the product owner, you should seldom overrule them, and never in sight of the team. In fact, unless you think they are headed towards utter disaster, it is often better to let the product owner go down their own path, even if it means they waste some time due to having to backtrack.

With this autonomy and authority comes a high level of responsibility. If the product owner gets final say, then they should be acting that way. That means they shouldn't be seeking approval as a means to protect themselves, or put together committees or seek input disguised as a way to shift blame if something goes awry. Making sure that product owners accept this responsibility is something that should be done explicitly, and any later actions that imply this isn't the case should be stopped.

The way that product owners and development teams interact is one of the critical changes that Agile brings with it. The product owner needs to be empowered, committed, and accountable. As the manager or leader of product owners, you must make sure that all three qualities are present and are lived by the people under your influence.

Choose product owners carefully. One of the easiest ways to have the product owners in your care succeed is to put them in a position of success. When choosing the product owner for a specific product or project, you need to take many factors into account. This not only includes their own skill and experience, but also the size of the project, the vertical or business area, as well as any challenges that you know the product owner will be facing.

This causes some difficult decisions to be made when determining appropriate staffing for a project. Some managers want to optimize for keeping teams together, moving entire teams from one project to the next. This allows for high-performing teams who have learned to work well together to keep the momentum going. Other managers view the role of product owner as a temporary one for the project only, and they have product managers play the roles in a rotational system as needed.

Both options have strengths and weaknesses. Some people are very good at being a product owner, but not nearly as good as being a product manager. The reverse can also be true; some people are very good at taking and improving an existing product, but launching a new one is beyond their abilities.

It's important for your organization to understand the staffing strategy that it wants to follow, and to understand the people that are available. Being sure to put someone in a position that aligns with their skills, experience and career aspirations is one of the easiest ways to put your team in a position to succeed.

Grant autonomy. As we discussed in a previous chapter, one strategy that managers attempt to use with new or inexperienced product owners is to put them on a short leash, or otherwise limit their freedom. This almost always leads to a bad result for the product, and a worse result for growing a new product owner.

A new product owner is likely to make plenty of mistakes, but these are important to the process. Not only does the product owner need to learn the job from doing it, but Agile also compensates for mistakes by allowing them to surface quickly and allow the team to change course if necessary. This doesn't mean completely let them flounder on their own; it means that as a senior manager, you should note that mistakes are bound to happen, and that they are almost always recoverable. The end result of a product owner who figures out how to get out of an error is both a stronger team and a stronger product owner. Do not get in the way of this kind of growth.

You can also expect a new product owner to take a little bit more time and effort to do the job properly. That means you must afford them the time they need in order to be effective. Being a product owner is often a full-time job; this is even truer for new product owners. Without enough available time to perform the duties that the team expects from them, a product owner will quickly lose credibility, and both product and product owner will suffer.

Build organizational support. The shift from traditional methods to Agile often comes with a lot of excitement and energy. There are seminars, change management activities, lunches, and maybe a fleece jacket or two. More than most other kinds of organizational change, the move to Agile requires ongoing support in the form of structures and a dedication to growth.

The first wave of product owners is likely to get a lot of training, outside resources and expert help. They will also be getting the most patience from the organization; everyone is new to the concepts, so people are more tolerant of mistakes. The challenge for senior management is to keep this momentum going, continue to provide training, time and patience for new product owners to join the ranks.

Those people in the first wave of Agile Product Owners should also be given the responsibility of helping to craft a community of improvement within the organization. This means crafting best practices, holding workshops and off-sites, and creating a management and mentorship program for the new people that come in.

Other topics for senior management include putting together the things that all employees need. Once the product owners feel like they understand their job, and are starting to get good at it, they are going to want to understand what their career path might be, and how they are going to be evaluated. This may cause a big change in review processes, or it might cause an entirely new method of judging success of employees. Every organization is different, but no organization can neglect this step, at least if it wants to keep a high-performing cadre of product owners functioning at a high level.

Made in United States
Troutdale, OR
10/26/2023

14034307R00086